Witches Get Riches

A Prosperity Magic Grimoire

Emeleth Morliniel

Woolmonger Publishing

Dedication

This one is for the regular working people who are hustling every day to make ends meet, but could use a little extra help. May Fortune smile upon you!

Table of Contents

Understanding Prosperity Magic

The Basics of Prosperity Magic

Prosperity magic encompasses a variety of practices aimed at attracting wealth and abundance into one's life. It draws upon the principles of intention, belief, and energy manipulation, which are foundational to many forms of witchcraft and spiritual practices. At its core, prosperity magic is about aligning one's personal energy with the flow of abundance in the universe, thereby creating a conducive environment for financial growth and opportunities. This subchapter will explore the essential elements of prosperity magic, including various spells, rituals, and tools that can be utilized for manifesting wealth.

One of the most popular methods within prosperity magic is the use of money spells. These spells can be simple or complex, often incorporating specific ingredients intended to amplify their effectiveness. Common components might include herbs known for their wealth-attracting properties, such as basil or cinnamon, and crystals like citrine or pyrite that are believed to enhance prosperity. An essential aspect of performing money spells is to set clear intentions and visualize the desired outcome, as these practices help to focus energy and align it with the universe's abundance.

Candle magic is another powerful practice for financial prosperity. Different colors of candles are associated with various types of energies; for example, green candles are often used for wealth and growth. By carving symbols or writing affirmations on the candle, practitioners can create a direct connection to their financial goals. Lighting the candle during specific moon phases, especially during the waxing moon, can further enhance the spell's effectiveness. Integrating visualization techniques during this process helps to solidify one's intentions and manifest them into reality.

Prosperity jars are a unique tool in the realm of abundance magic, allowing practitioners to create a physical representation of their financial goals. These jars can be filled with various items, such as coins, herbs, and personal affirmations, all meant to attract wealth. Once created, the jar serves as a constant reminder of one's intentions and can be placed on an altar or in a prominent location within the home. Regularly focusing on the jar, especially during rituals or meditations, reinforces the intention and invites the energy of abundance into one's life.

Energy clearing is a vital component of prosperity magic, as financial blockages can often stem from negative beliefs or past experiences. Techniques such as smudging with sage, using sound healing, or performing rituals during specific moon phases can help clear these obstacles. Incorporating divination practices, such as tarot readings or pendulum work, can provide insight into one's financial situation and highlight areas where energy may be stagnant. By actively engaging in these practices, individuals can cultivate a mindset of abundance, making room for new opportunities and financial growth.

The Role of Intention in Manifesting Money

The concept of intention is fundamental in the practice of manifesting money, particularly within the realms of prosperity magic and witchcraft. Intention acts as the guiding force that aligns your desires with the universe's energies. When you set a clear and focused intention, you create a powerful energetic signal that communicates your desires to the universe. This clarity is essential; it helps you define what wealth means to you, whether it's a specific amount of money, financial freedom, or the ability to invest in your passions. Without a clear intention, the energy you send out can become muddled, leading to less effective manifestations.

Incorporating intention into your money manifestation rituals can take various forms. For example, when performing a candle magic spell for financial prosperity, lighting a green candle can symbolize growth and abundance. As you light the candle, articulate your intention aloud, visualizing your financial goals as if they are already a reality. This practice not only enhances your focus but also embeds your desires into the energetic realm. The more specific and heartfelt your intention, the stronger the energy you generate, which can attract opportunities and resources that align with your financial aspirations.

Crystals also play a vital role in intention setting for wealth attraction. Selecting stones like citrine or pyrite, known for their money-attracting properties, allows you to enhance your intentions. By holding the crystal while visualizing your financial goals, you create a tangible link between your intentions and the energies of the stone. Additionally, placing these crystals on your prosperity altar while stating your intentions can amplify the vibrational frequency of abundance in your environment. This practice reinforces your commitment and aligns your subconscious mind with your conscious desires.

Moreover, the phases of the moon can significantly influence the effectiveness of your intentions. New moons are ideal for setting intentions and initiating new ventures, while full moons are perfect for releasing what no longer serves you, including financial doubts or blocks. Engaging in moon phase rituals allows you to harness the natural rhythms of the universe, further enhancing your ability to manifest wealth. By aligning your intentions with these lunar cycles, you tap into a powerful source of energy that supports your financial growth.

Intention should not solely focus on the end result but also on the journey and the energy you cultivate along the way. Utilizing abundance affirmations and visualization techniques reinforces your intention daily, helping shift your mindset towards receptivity and gratitude. Engaging in practices like herbal sachets and prosperity jars can serve as physical reminders of your intentions, keeping your focus sharp. By integrating these diverse methods into your manifestation practice, you create a holistic approach that nurtures your financial goals and invites prosperity into your life.

Common Misconceptions About Wealth and Witchcraft

Wealth and witchcraft are often viewed through a lens of misunderstanding that can hinder the practice of prosperity magic. A prevalent misconception is that witchcraft inherently promotes greed or materialism. On the contrary, many witches see wealth not merely as a measure of financial success but as a tool for achieving greater good, enabling them to support their communities, fund projects, and create positive change in the world. This distinction is crucial; wealth becomes a means of empowerment rather than an end goal, aligning with the ethical principles of many spiritual paths.

Another common belief is that wealth can be manifested without any effort or responsibility. While rituals and spells, such as those involving crystals or candle magic, can enhance one's ability to attract abundance, they are most effective when combined with practical actions. Manifestation is not about waiting for riches to fall from the sky; it requires a commitment to setting clear intentions, taking actionable steps, and maintaining a positive mindset. Rituals serve as catalysts, helping to align one's energy with their financial goals, but they should be paired with diligent work and strategic planning.

Some skeptics argue that prosperity magic is merely a form of wishful thinking, dismissing it as a frivolous or outdated practice. However, many practitioners find that rituals like moon phase ceremonies, prosperity jars, and herbal sachets serve to reinforce their intentions and focus their energy on financial growth. These methods are rooted in ancient traditions and are often supported by contemporary spiritual practices. The energy and symbolism involved in these rituals can create a powerful framework that encourages a proactive approach to money, allowing individuals to tap into their own potential for abundance.

Additionally, there is a misconception that only certain types of people can effectively practice financial witchcraft. Many believe that wealth attraction spells are reserved for the privileged or those with specialized knowledge. In reality, prosperity magic is accessible to everyone, regardless of their background or financial status. Techniques like abundance affirmations, visualization, and energy clearing can be adapted to suit each individual's circumstances. The beauty of these practices lies in their versatility; they can empower anyone, from entrepreneurs to working-class individuals, to cultivate a mindset and environment conducive to attracting wealth.

Some may think that financial prosperity and spiritual growth are mutually exclusive. This belief can create a barrier to those seeking to integrate their spiritual practices with their financial aspirations. In truth, wealth and spirituality can coexist harmoniously. Many spiritual seekers find that their financial growth enhances their ability to contribute to their communities and support their spiritual journeys. By embracing the interconnectedness of these aspects, individuals can develop a holistic approach to prosperity that honors both their material and spiritual needs, leading to a more fulfilling and abundant life.

Money Spells and Rituals

Introduction to Money Spells

Money spells have long held a place in the practice of witchcraft, serving as a bridge between the spiritual and material realms. In contemporary society, where financial stability often feels elusive, many practitioners turn to these rituals to manifest prosperity and abundance. This subchapter will explore the foundational principles of money spells, their historical context, and how they resonate with the desires of modern seekers. Whether you identify as a witch, a pagan, or simply someone searching for ways to enhance your financial situation, understanding these spells can empower you to harness their energy effectively.

At its core, a money spell is a focused intention set with the goal of attracting wealth or enhancing financial opportunities. The essence of witchcraft lies in the belief that our thoughts and energies can influence the world around us. By channeling this energy through specific rituals, practitioners aim to align their vibrational frequency with that of prosperity. This alignment can manifest in various forms, from unexpected financial windfalls to new job opportunities or successful business ventures. The process often involves a combination of visualization techniques, affirmations, and the use of symbolic tools like candles, crystals, and herbs.

Crystals, in particular, play a significant role in money spells. Each stone carries unique properties that can enhance the energy of a spell. For instance, citrine is known as the "merchant's stone," believed to attract wealth and success. Similarly, green aventurine is celebrated for its ability to promote luck and abundance. Incorporating these crystals into your rituals can amplify your intentions and create a powerful energy field that encourages financial growth. It's essential to cleanse and charge your crystals regularly to maintain their effectiveness and ensure they resonate with your specific goals.

Candle magic is another popular method for those seeking financial prosperity. Different colors symbolize various aspects of abundance, with green often representing prosperity and success. By lighting candles during a spell, practitioners can enhance their focus and intention, creating a vibrant atmosphere conducive to manifesting wealth. Additionally, incorporating herbal sachets filled with plants known for their money-attracting properties can further enrich your spellwork. Herbs like basil, mint, and cinnamon are traditionally used for their potent associations with prosperity and can be easily integrated into your rituals.

Understanding lunar cycles can significantly impact the effectiveness of your money spells. Specific moon phases are believed to be more favorable for certain types of manifestations, with the waxing moon being ideal for attracting new opportunities. Engaging in rituals during these times can enhance your results and align your efforts with the natural rhythms of the universe. By incorporating prosperity jars, divination practices, and energy-clearing techniques into your spellwork, you can cultivate a holistic approach to financial manifestation that resonates with your personal journey toward abundance.

Colors and Their Meanings for Prosperity Magic

Colors play a pivotal role in prosperity rituals, influencing the energy and intention behind our magical practices. Each color carries its own vibration and symbolism, which can enhance the effectiveness of rituals aimed at attracting wealth and abundance. Understanding the significance of these colors allows practitioners to strategically incorporate them into their spells, affirmations, and visualizations. This knowledge can transform a routine ritual into a powerful act of manifestation, making it essential for anyone interested in prosperity magic.

Green is perhaps the most recognized color

associated with prosperity and abundance. It represents growth, renewal, and fertility, making it ideal for rituals focused on financial gain and success. Incorporating green candles, crystals such as aventurine or emerald, or even green herbs like basil into spells can amplify the energy of attraction. The vibrational frequency of green resonates with the heart chakra, promoting feelings of openness and receptivity, essential for inviting wealth into one's life.

Gold is another powerful color linked to prosperity. It symbolizes wealth, success, and achievement. Utilizing gold candles or decorations in rituals can evoke a sense of luxury and abundance. Gold is often associated with the sun, representing vitality and energy, which can catalyze financial growth. When combined with affirmations or visualization techniques, gold can elevate the practitioner's intent, reinforcing beliefs in their capability to achieve financial goals and manifest their desires.

Red, while often associated with passion and power, also holds significance in prosperity rituals. It embodies strength, courage, and determination, qualities essential for entrepreneurs and those seeking financial independence. Incorporating red into rituals can help practitioners overcome financial obstacles and take decisive action toward their goals. Whether through red candles, crystals like garnet, or red herbs such as cinnamon, this color can ignite the willpower needed for financial success.

Blue and purple also play significant roles in prosperity magic. Blue often symbolizes stability and trust, which are crucial for building strong financial foundations. It can help practitioners attract opportunities that align with their values and long-term goals. Purple, associated with intuition and spiritual insight, enhances the ability to make wise financial decisions and recognize abundance in all forms. By understanding and utilizing these colors intentionally, practitioners can create a multi-faceted approach to prosperity rituals, enhancing their effectiveness and deepening their connection to the energies of wealth and abundance.

Popular Money Spells for Beginners

Popular money spells for beginners often serve as accessible entry points into the world of prosperity magic. These practices are designed to attract wealth and abundance into one's life without requiring extensive experience or elaborate rituals. For those new to this realm, simple spells can be performed using everyday materials and intentions, making them perfect for busy individuals, entrepreneurs, and spiritual seekers alike. By focusing on their desires and aligning their energy with the universe, practitioners can begin to shift their financial circumstances in a positive direction.

One of the most popular spells for beginners is the use of prosperity jars. These jars are filled with various ingredients that symbolize wealth and abundance, such as coins, herbs like basil or cinnamon, and any personal items that resonate with prosperity. Once assembled, the jar is charged with intention, often placed in a prominent location in the home or workspace. This tangible reminder of one's goals serves to keep the energy of abundance flowing and acts as a beacon for attracting financial opportunities.

Candle magic is another straightforward yet powerful method for manifesting wealth. By selecting colors associated with prosperity, such as green or gold, practitioners can create a simple ritual that involves lighting a candle while focusing on their financial goals. Affirmations can be recited during this process to reinforce the intention. The flame acts as a conduit for energy, helping to amplify the spell's effectiveness as it burns. This practice can easily be integrated into a weekly routine, making it especially appealing to busy individuals seeking consistent financial growth.

Herbal sachets are also an excellent option for those looking to attract wealth. By combining herbs known for their prosperity-enhancing properties, such as chamomile, mint, or ginger, practitioners can create small sachets to carry with them or place in their home. These sachets can be charged with personal intentions, and their presence serves as a constant reminder of one's financial aspirations. This method not only promotes abundance but also allows for creativity in choosing herbs that resonate personally with the practitioner.

Moon phase rituals can enhance one's financial manifestations. Each lunar phase offers unique energies that can be harnessed for specific intentions. For example, the new moon is ideal for setting intentions and planting seeds for future growth, while the full moon is perfect for gratitude and releasing any limiting beliefs about money. By aligning financial goals with the lunar cycle, practitioners can tap into the natural rhythms of the universe, enhancing the potency of their spells and rituals. This approach empowers individuals to take charge of their financial destinies while fostering a deeper connection with nature.

Green Candle Money Attraction Spell
Materials Needed:
- A small green candle
- A coin (preferably a high-denomination one)
- Basil or cinnamon essential oil
- A small piece of paper
- Pen
Instructions:
1. Carve your name and the amount of money you wish to attract into the candle.

2. Anoint the candle with the essential oil, envisioning your goal as you do.
3. Write your financial goal on the piece of paper and place it under the candle.
4. Place the coin next to the paper.
5. Light the candle and focus on the flame, visualizing your financial success.
6. Let the candle burn completely while maintaining your intention.
7. Keep the coin in your wallet as a token of the spell.

Money Attracting Sachet
Materials:
- A small green bag or pouch
- A handful of basil, mint, and chamomile
- A few drops of bergamot essential oil
- A small citrine crystal
Instructions:
1. Gather the herbs and place them in the green pouch.
2. Add the citrine crystal.
3. Drop a few drops of bergamot oil onto the herbs, imagining riches flowing into your life.
4. Seal the pouch and hold it in your hands, stating your intention clearly for financial abundance.
5. Place the sachet in your home or carry it with you to attract prosperity.

Money Bowl Spell

Materials:

- A small bowl

- High-denomination coins and paper money

- Bay leaves

- A sprinkle of cinnamon

- Gold or green glitter

Instructions:

1. Place the coins and money in the bowl.

2. Add bay leaves, saying, "As these leaves are abundant, so will my wealth grow."

3. Sprinkle cinnamon into the bowl, affirming prosperity and financial security.

4. Add a touch of glitter to symbolize the sparkle of newfound wealth.

5. Place the bowl in a prominent area and focus on it regularly to reinforce your wealth intentions.

Lucky Dice Number Casting

Materials Needed:

- Two six-sided dice

- A journal or notebook

- A quiet space

Instructions:

1. Sit quietly and focus on the lottery draw you wish to participate in while holding the dice.

2. Roll the dice three times, recording the outcomes of each roll.

3. Use the totals from each roll to inspire your lottery numbers. For example, if you rolled a 4 and a 5, your first lottery number could be 9.

4. After rolling, reflect on any patterns or feelings you experienced during the rolls to guide your final choice of numbers.

5. Write down your selected numbers in the journal, along with a note about why you chose them based on the dice rolls, and keep this journal visible for regular inspiration.

Prosperity Visualization Spell

Materials:

- A comfortable, quiet space
- A piece of paper and pen

Instructions:

1. Sit peacefully and close your eyes, taking deep breaths to center yourself.

2. Visualize money and prosperity flowing effortlessly into your life.

3. Feel the emotion of receiving wealth—joy, security, freedom.

4. Open your eyes and write down the feelings and images that came to you.

5. Keep this paper in a place where you can frequently revisit it to reinforce your manifestation.

Moonlight Abundance Ritual

Materials:

- A bowl of water
- A small bowl of salt
- A piece of paper
- A pen

Instructions:

1. On the night of a full moon, place the bowl of water outside (or by a window) to absorb the moonlight.

2. Write down what you want to attract in terms of abundance on the piece of paper.

3. Sprinkle a pinch of salt into the water while saying a positive affirmation regarding abundance.

4. Let the water soak up the moonlight overnight, then use it to wash your hands or sprinkle around your home for enhanced abundance energy.

Golden Thread Wealth Spell

Materials Needed:

- A piece of green or gold thread
- Three coins of different denominations
- A small pouch or bag

Instructions:

1. Sit in a quiet space and take the thread, tying a knot around each coin while stating an intention like, "With this coin, my wealth multiplies."

2. After tying all three coins, visualize your financial goals as you hold the threaded coins.

3. Place the threaded coins into the pouch.

4. Carry the pouch with you, or store it in a place related to your finances, like a desk or safe, to continually draw in wealth.

Prosperity Plant Ritual

Materials Needed:

- A plant pot
- Soil
- Seeds of a fast-growing plant (like basil or mint)
- A small obsidian or jade stone

Instructions:

1. Fill the pot with soil, holding your intention of financial growth and prosperity.
2. Plant the seeds, saying, "As these seeds grow, so does my fortune."
3. Place the stone in the soil for protection and grounding of your intentions.
4. Care for the plant regularly, visualizing your financial situation flourishing as the plant grows.

Mirror Wealth Manifestation Spell

Materials:

- A small mirror
- Gold or yellow candle
- A prosperity affirmation

Instructions:

1. Sit in front of the mirror and light the candle.
2. Look into your reflection, envisioning a prosperous version of yourself.

3. Recite the prosperity affirmation aloud, focusing on your intent: "I reflect abundance and wealth flows to me."

4. Allow the candle to burn while keeping your eyes on your reflection and feeling the reality of your affirmation.

5. Use this mirror for future prosperity work to reinforce your goals.

Creating Your Own Money Spell

Creating your own money spell is an empowering process that invites you to harness your personal energy and intention to attract prosperity into your life. The first step in crafting a money spell is to clearly define your financial goals. Whether you seek a stable income, a new job, or simply a boost in your financial situation, having a specific intention will focus your energy and increase the spell's effectiveness. Take time to meditate on what abundance means to you, and write down your desires in a clear and concise manner. This written intention will serve as the foundation of your spell.

Next, selecting the right materials can enhance your spell's potency. Crystals such as citrine, pyrite, and green aventurine are known for their wealth-attracting properties. Consider incorporating these stones into your ritual, either by placing them on your altar or carrying them with you. Additionally, using herbs like basil, cinnamon, and mint can create powerful sachets that draw in financial energy. Gather these materials with intention, allowing your excitement and hope for abundance to infuse them with your desires.

Candle magic is another effective technique for manifesting financial prosperity. Choose a green or gold candle to symbolize money and abundance. As you light the candle, visualize your financial goals coming to fruition. You can carve symbols or words related to your intention into the candle's wax, further personalizing your spell. Allow the candle to burn for a set amount of time each day, reinforcing your intention and keeping your focus on attracting wealth. The flame serves as a beacon, drawing in the energy of abundance.

Integrating affirmations and visualization techniques into your spell can amplify its effects. Create affirmations that resonate with you, such as "I am open to receiving wealth" or "Abundance flows to me effortlessly." Repeat these affirmations daily, ideally while visualizing the financial success you desire. This combination of positive affirmations and mental imagery helps align your mindset with your goals, making it easier for you to recognize opportunities for growth in your life.

Consider incorporating moon phase rituals into your money spell. The waxing moon is an ideal time for attracting new opportunities and abundance, while the full moon can be a powerful moment for gratitude and reflection on your financial journey. You might also create a prosperity jar filled with coins, herbs, and crystals, sealing it with your intention written on a piece of paper. This jar acts as a physical representation of your spell and can be placed on your altar or in a special spot in your home. By combining these elements, you create a personalized and potent money spell that aligns with your unique energy and intentions, paving the way for financial growth and abundance in your life.

Creating a Prosperity Altar

Selecting a Space

Selecting the right location for your altar is crucial in enhancing your practice of prosperity magic. The space you choose will not only influence the energy you cultivate but also serve as a reflection of your intentions. Ideally, your altar should be a place where you feel comfortable, focused, and inspired. Consider areas in your home that naturally draw your attention or where you often find yourself daydreaming about abundance and wealth. A quiet corner of a room, a dedicated shelf, or even a small table can become a powerful spot for your rituals and manifestations.

When evaluating potential locations, think about the energy flow in your home. Spaces that are cluttered or chaotic may hinder your ability to concentrate and connect with your intentions. Look for areas that are well-lit, preferably with natural light, as this can enhance the vibrational frequency of your altar. Additionally, consider the direction the space faces; south and southeast are traditionally associated with wealth and abundance in many spiritual practices. A location that resonates with these energies will amplify your rituals and help you align with your financial goals.

Another important factor is accessibility. Your altar should be easily reachable, allowing you to engage with it regularly. This accessibility encourages a consistent practice, whether it's performing money spells, lighting candles for financial prosperity, or creating prosperity jars. If your altar is tucked away in a seldom-used room, you might find it challenging to connect with your daily or weekly rituals. Make sure the space invites you in and allows for spontaneous moments of reflection or action when inspiration strikes.

You should also consider the aesthetics of your chosen location. The visual appeal of your altar can significantly impact your emotional and energetic response. Decorate your space with items that resonate with your intentions, such as crystals for wealth attraction, herbs for abundance sachets, or symbols and images that reflect your goals. Personalizing your altar not only makes the space inviting but also strengthens your connection to the energies you're working with. Remember, a well-curated altar serves as a visual reminder of your journey toward prosperity.

Ensure that your chosen space is clear of negative energies or distractions. Regularly cleanse the area with herbs, crystals, or sound to maintain a high vibrational atmosphere. This energy clearing practice can help eliminate any financial blockages and create a more conducive environment for your prosperity magic. By thoughtfully selecting a location for your altar, you establish a sacred space that supports your desires, enhances your rituals, and aids in manifesting the wealth and abundance you seek.

What to Include on Your Prosperity Altar

Creating a prosperity altar is an essential step for anyone seeking to manifest abundance and financial growth in their life. A well-curated altar serves as a focal point for your intentions and aligns your energy with the vibrations of wealth. When setting up your prosperity altar, it's vital to include items that resonate with your personal beliefs while also enhancing your connection to prosperity magic. Start with a clean space that feels inviting and sacred, as this will set the tone for your practices.

One of the foundational items for any prosperity altar is crystals. Certain stones are believed to attract wealth and abundance, such as citrine, pyrite, and green aventurine. These crystals can be placed in a small dish or scattered around the altar. Additionally, incorporating gold or green candles can amplify your intentions during rituals. Lighting candles while focusing on your financial goals can create a powerful atmosphere conducive to manifestation. Remember to choose colors that represent abundance for you, as personal significance can enhance the energy you work with.

Herbal elements are also significant in prosperity magic. Consider adding sachets filled with herbs like basil, cinnamon, and mint, which are traditionally associated with wealth attraction. These sachets can be placed on your altar or carried with you to continually draw in prosperity. Another useful item is a prosperity jar, which you can fill with ingredients that symbolize your financial goals, such as coins, seeds, and written affirmations. This jar can serve as a physical representation of your intentions and can be charged during rituals to enhance its power.

Incorporating divination tools can provide insights into your financial journey. Tarot cards or an oracle deck can be included on your altar to help you navigate your path to prosperity. You can draw cards during your rituals to gain clarity on financial decisions or to understand any blockages that might be present. Additionally, charms and talismans crafted for abundance can be placed on the altar to further amplify your manifestation efforts. These items can be personalized to reflect your unique aspirations, making your altar a true reflection of your desires.

Energy clearing tools such as sage, palo santo, or sound bowls can be vital in maintaining a clear and receptive space for prosperity. Regularly cleansing your altar helps to remove any stagnant energy that may hinder your financial growth. Coupling this practice with moon phase rituals, particularly during the new moon for setting intentions and the full moon for releasing blockages, can enhance your prosperity magic. By thoughtfully selecting items for your altar, you create a powerful space that not only reflects your goals but actively supports your journey toward financial abundance.

Consecration and Dedication

Consecration and dedication are essential practices for anyone looking to empower their altar space, especially within the realms of prosperity magic and abundance rituals. These rituals serve to cleanse and charge your altar with intention, creating an environment conducive to attracting wealth and prosperity. Start by selecting a time that resonates with you, perhaps during a new moon or on a day associated with abundance, such as Thursday. Gather your tools—candles, crystals, herbs, and any other items you plan to use. As you prepare your space, approach the process with a clear mind and a focused intention, allowing your energy to flow into the ritual.

Cleansing your altar is the first step in the consecration process. This might involve smudging with sage or palo santo to remove any negative energies or lingering influences. As you cleanse, visualize any blockages dissipating, making way for positive energy. You can also use salt and water or sound, such as a bell or singing bowl, to purify the space. This physical and energetic cleaning sets the stage for the powerful work you will do. Remember, a clean space invites fresh opportunities and abundance into your life.

Once your altar is cleansed, it's time to dedicate it to your intentions. This can be done through a spoken affirmation or a written declaration. Speak or write about your goals, desires, and the energy you wish to attract. You might say, "I dedicate this space to the manifestation of wealth and abundance in my life." As you do this, hold your chosen crystals—like citrine for prosperity or green aventurine for growth—in your hands, allowing their energies to enhance your intentions. The act of dedication imbues your altar with purpose, making it a focal point for your prosperity spells and rituals.

Incorporating rituals tailored to your specific goals can further empower your altar space. For instance, candle magic is a potent tool for financial prosperity. Choose candles in colors that correspond to your desires—green for wealth, gold for success—and anoint them with oils that resonate with abundance, such as cinnamon or patchouli. As you light these candles, visualize your financial goals coming to fruition. Additionally, creating prosperity jars filled with herbs, coins, and affirmations can serve as a powerful reminder of your intentions, enhancing the energy of your altar.

Regularly clearing energy is key to maintaining the vibrancy of your altar space. Over time, stagnant energy can accumulate, potentially hindering your prosperity efforts. Incorporate moon phase rituals to reset your intentions, using the waxing moon for growth and the full moon for gratitude. Engage in divination practices to gain insight into your financial journey and to refine your goals. By consistently dedicating time to your altar and utilizing these empowering rituals, you can create a sacred space that not only supports your financial aspirations but also nurtures your overall abundance mindset.

Abundance Affirmations and Visualization Techniques

The Power of Affirmations

The power of affirmations lies in their ability to reshape our thoughts and beliefs about wealth and prosperity. For many, the concept of abundance can feel distant or unattainable, but affirmations serve as a bridge to transforming that mindset. By consistently repeating positive statements about money and prosperity, individuals can rewire their subconscious, replacing limiting beliefs with empowering ones. This practice is especially valuable for witches and spiritual seekers who wish to enhance their money manifestation rituals and align their energy with the flow of abundance.

When crafting affirmations, it is essential to focus on clarity and positivity. Phrases like "I attract wealth effortlessly" or "Money flows to me from unexpected sources" can be powerful tools for those in the working class or entrepreneurial spaces. These affirmations not only strengthen the belief in one's ability to create financial success but also align with various practices within prosperity magic. By integrating affirmations into daily routines, such as during meditation or while lighting a candle for financial prosperity, practitioners can amplify their intentions and reinforce their commitment to attracting abundance.

Moreover, the effectiveness of affirmations can be heightened through visualization techniques. When combined, affirmations and visualization create a potent synergy that further embeds the desired reality into the subconscious mind. For instance, visualizing oneself in a state of financial freedom while repeating affirmations can enhance emotional engagement and clarity of intent. This technique is especially appealing to Millennials and Gen Z, who often seek practical and relatable ways to manifest their desires through both modern and traditional practices.

Incorporating affirmations into other prosperity rituals can also deepen their impact. For instance, placing written affirmations in prosperity jars or herbal sachets can serve as a constant reminder of one's financial goals. Similarly, using charms and talismans inscribed with affirmations can enhance the energy surrounding one's wealth attraction efforts. The moon phases can also play a crucial role;

during the waxing phase, practitioners can focus on affirmations related to growth and abundance, while the full moon can be a time to celebrate and express gratitude for the wealth already received.

Affirmations work best when paired with energy clearing practices. Addressing financial blockages—be they emotional, psychological, or spiritual—can create a clearer path for abundance to flow into one's life. By regularly engaging in divination practices for financial insight, witches and spiritual seekers can identify and release any limiting beliefs that may hinder their relationship with money. Embracing the power of affirmations alongside these various tools creates a holistic approach to prosperity magic, enabling individuals to cultivate a mindset that attracts wealth and nurtures abundance.

Crafting Effective Abundance Affirmations

Crafting effective abundance affirmations is a powerful practice that aligns your mindset with your financial goals and aspirations. Affirmations serve as a bridge between your current reality and the prosperous life you envision. To create affirmations that resonate deeply with you, start by identifying your specific financial desires. Whether you seek increased income, financial freedom, or a sense of security, your affirmations should reflect these aspirations clearly and positively. Use present tense language to convey that these goals are already in motion, reinforcing a mindset of abundance.

When formulating your affirmations, focus on emotional resonance. Words hold power, and the emotions they evoke can significantly impact your manifestation process. Choose phrases that not only articulate your desires but also inspire feelings of joy, gratitude, and empowerment. For example, rather than stating, "I want to be wealthy," consider affirming, "I am grateful for the financial abundance flowing into my life." This subtle shift in wording creates a more positive and affirmative statement, enhancing its effectiveness.

Incorporating visualization techniques can further amplify the power of your affirmations. As you recite them, envision your desired outcome vividly. Picture yourself living in a state of abundance, experiencing the joy and freedom that comes with it. Engage all your senses in this visualization; imagine the sights, sounds, and feelings associated with your financial success. This mental imagery, combined with your affirmations, creates a potent manifestation tool that aligns your energy with your goals, making it easier to attract opportunities and resources.

Utilizing crystals in conjunction with your affirmations can also enhance your prosperity magic. Certain crystals, such as citrine and pyrite, are well-known for their wealth-attracting properties.

Hold these crystals while reciting your affirmations, or place them in a dedicated prosperity jar along with written affirmations. This physical representation of your intentions not only serves as a reminder of your goals but also amplifies the energy of your affirmations, creating a harmonious environment for attracting abundance.

Integrating your affirmations into daily rituals can establish a consistent practice that reinforces your intentions. Consider lighting a candle while reciting your affirmations, allowing the flame to symbolize the illumination of your financial path. Alternatively, create an herbal sachet filled with prosperity herbs, and include your affirmations inside. By embedding your affirmations into tangible practices, you create a multi-sensory experience that deepens your connection to your financial goals, making the journey toward abundance both magical and transformative.

Here are some examples of powerful affirmations designed to attract money and prosperity into your life:

"I am a magnet for abundance and prosperity flows effortlessly into my life."

"Money comes to me in expected and unexpected ways, filling my life with joy and security."

"I am worthy of financial success and embrace the opportunities that come my way."

"I attract wealth and abundance through my positive

thoughts and actions."

"Every day, I am becoming more financially secure and confident in my abilities."

"I release all limiting beliefs about money and open myself to infinite possibilities."

"I am grateful for the financial resources I have and trust that more is on its way."

"I create and embrace opportunities to generate wealth and enhance my prosperity."

Adapt these affirmations to align more closely with your personal circumstances or resonate better with your aspirations. Repeat them daily, either aloud or in writing, to reinforce a mindset of abundance and attract prosperity

Visualization Techniques for Financial Success

Visualization techniques are powerful tools that can help individuals align their intentions with their financial goals. For those in the realms of witchcraft and spiritual practice, visualization goes beyond mere daydreaming; it becomes an act of manifestation. By creating a clear mental image of financial success, practitioners can harness the energy of their intentions, making it easier to attract abundance into their lives. This practice is not just about seeing the end result, but also about feeling the emotions associated with achieving those goals, which amplifies the energy being sent out into the universe.

One effective visualization technique involves

creating a vision board dedicated to financial prosperity. This board can be filled with images, words, and symbols that resonate with one's financial aspirations. For instance, including images of the lifestyle one wishes to lead, such as dream homes or luxurious experiences, helps to create a tangible connection to those desires. By spending time each day focusing on this board, practitioners can reinforce their intentions and keep their financial goals at the forefront of their minds. This daily practice can be enhanced through meditation or candle magic, where the light of the candle symbolizes the illumination of one's path to wealth.

Incorporating crystals into visualization practices can elevate the effectiveness of these techniques. Crystals such as citrine, green aventurine, and pyrite are known for their properties of attracting wealth and prosperity. Holding or placing these crystals on your vision board while visualizing your financial success can help to amplify the energy of your intentions. Additionally, pairing this with abundance affirmations can create a powerful synergy. Affirmations should be positive, present-tense statements that reinforce the belief in one's ability to attract wealth, such as "I am open to receiving abundance in all forms."

The lunar cycle offers a unique opportunity to enhance visualization techniques through specific moon phase rituals. New moons are ideal for setting intentions, while full moons can be used for gratitude and reflection on the abundance already received. Practitioners can create rituals that include visualizations during these lunar phases, focusing on what they wish to manifest. This connection to the natural rhythms of the universe can provide a deeper sense of alignment and purpose, making financial goals feel more attainable and supported by the energies of the cosmos.

Including divination practices such as tarot or pendulum work can provide insight into financial blockages and opportunities. By using these tools in conjunction with visualization techniques, practitioners can gain clarity on their financial paths. This holistic approach not only focuses on the act of visualization but also addresses any subconscious beliefs or fears that may be hindering financial success. Through consistent practice of these techniques, individuals can effectively clear energetic blockages and create a more abundant reality, transforming their financial landscape with intention and magic.

Vision Board Lottery Ritual

Materials Needed:

- A poster board or cork board
- Magazines, printed images, or drawings
- Glue or pins
- Markers

Instructions:
1. Gather materials that represent your dreams of winning the lottery and achieving financial freedom (e.g., images of money, vacations, new homes).
2. Dedicate a section of the board specifically to your lottery numbers. Choose numbers that resonate with you or that you've felt drawn to in the past.
3. Create a vision board by arranging your images and numbers in a way that feels inspiring to you. Use markers to decorate or enhance your numbers with positive affirmations about luck and abundance.
4. Place your vision board in a prominent place where you will see it daily, reinforcing your intention to attract winning lottery numbers and good fortune.
5. Spend a few minutes each day visualizing your success as you look at the board, feeling gratitude for the abundance you're inviting into your life.

Abundance Affirmation Ritual
Materials:
- Mirror
- A list of affirmations related to money and success
Instructions:
1. Choose a quiet place and stand in front of the mirror.
2. Recite your affirmations out loud with confidence, looking directly at yourself. Phrases like "I attract

wealth" or "Abundance flows to me effortlessly" work well.

3. Repeat your affirmations daily or weekly. You can also write them down and place them near your mirror as a reminder.

Wealthy Lifestyle Vision Board

Materials Needed:

- A large poster board or cork board
- Magazines or printouts reflecting luxury items and lifestyles
- Scissors
- Glue or pins

Instructions:

1. Cut out images, words, and phrases that resonate with the luxurious life you desire.
2. Arrange the cutouts on the board in a way that feels appealing and inspiring to you.
3. As you glue down each item, visualize yourself living that luxury and comfort, enhancing the feelings of abundance.
4. Place the vision board in a prominent area of your home where you can see it daily.
5. Spend time gazing at the board each day, reinforcing the beliefs that you deserve this lifestyle.

Luxury Bath Spell

Materials Needed:

- A bathtub or large bowl

- Sea salt or Epsom salt
- Essential oils (ylang-ylang or sandalwood)
- Flower petals (like roses or jasmine)

Instructions:

1. Fill the bathtub or bowl with warm water. As you do, visualize your ideal luxurious life.

2. Add a generous amount of sea salt or Epsom salt to the water, focusing on cleansing away financial blocks.

3. Drop in the essential oils and flower petals, visualizing their fragrance enveloping you in comfort and luxury.

4. Soak in the bath, repeating affirmations like, "I am worthy of luxury and comfort."

5. After your bath, feel the relaxation and abundance you've attracted, and allow the water to carry away any lingering stress.

Crystal Magic for Wealth Attraction

How Crystals Attract Wealth

Crystals have long been revered for their energetic properties and ability to influence various aspects of life, including wealth and prosperity. The belief that certain stones can attract financial abundance is rooted in both ancient traditions and modern practices. Each crystal carries a unique vibration that interacts with the energy of the user, allowing practitioners to align their intentions with the frequencies of wealth and success. By incorporating these stones into wealth attraction rituals, individuals tap into their potential to manifest financial growth and opportunities.

Among the most popular crystals for attracting wealth are citrine, pyrite, and green aventurine. Citrine, often referred to as the "merchant's stone," is believed to promote success and abundance in business endeavors. Its sunny yellow hue reflects positivity and the energy of wealth. Pyrite, known as "fool's gold," symbolizes abundance and is thought to attract prosperity while warding off negative energy. Green aventurine, often considered the "stone of opportunity," is linked to luck and is a favorite among those seeking to enhance their financial prospects. By carrying, wearing, or placing these crystals in strategic locations, practitioners can enhance their financial intentions.

To maximize the effectiveness of wealth-attracting crystals, individuals can integrate them into their money manifestation rituals. This may involve creating a sacred space with the chosen crystals, lighting candles that correspond to prosperity, and reciting abundance affirmations aloud. Visualization techniques play a crucial role in this process. Practitioners are encouraged to envision their financial goals vividly while holding the crystals, allowing the energy of the stones to amplify their intentions. This synergy between intention and crystal energy can create a powerful magnet for financial opportunities.

In addition to personal rituals, crystals can also be incorporated into group practices or community events focused on prosperity. Many witches and spiritual seekers gather to perform collective rituals, sharing their energy and intentions for wealth. Creating prosperity jars filled with crystals, herbs, and other symbols of abundance can serve as a tangible focus for collective manifestation efforts.

These jars can be placed on altars or carried during rituals, symbolizing the power of community in attracting wealth and supporting one another's financial goals.

Maintain a clear and open energy flow to fully benefit from the properties of wealth-attracting crystals. Regular energy clearing practices, such as smudging with herbs, using sound, or bathing crystals in moonlight, can help remove any blockages that may hinder prosperity. By nurturing both the physical and energetic aspects of wealth attraction, practitioners can create a harmonious environment conducive to financial growth. The integration of crystals into prosperity magic is not merely about the stones themselves but about the intentions and actions that accompany their use.

Crystals for Wealth

Crystals have long been associated with various forms of magic, including those aimed at attracting wealth and prosperity. Among the most powerful crystals for wealth are citrine, pyrite, green aventurine, and clear quartz. Each of these stones carries unique properties that can enhance your financial situation and help manifest abundance. For instance, citrine, often referred to as the "merchant's stone," is known for its ability to attract wealth and success. Carrying a piece of citrine or placing it in your workspace can create an atmosphere conducive to financial growth. Similarly, pyrite, with its metallic luster, not only attracts wealth but also encourages confidence and assertiveness in financial dealings.

Green aventurine is another essential crystal for abundance, often called the "stone of opportunity." It is believed to enhance luck, particularly in financial ventures. To harness its energy, you can carry green aventurine in your pocket or wear it as jewelry while performing money manifestation rituals. Additionally, placing it in your cash drawer or wallet can amplify its effects. Clear quartz, known as a master healer, is excellent for amplifying the energies of other crystals. Incorporating clear quartz into your wealth rituals can enhance your intentions, making your money spells more potent.

To effectively use these crystals, consider incorporating them into your daily practice. You can create a prosperity jar filled with these stones, along with herbs and affirmations that resonate with your financial goals. Each time you add to the jar, visualize your intentions manifesting. For a more dynamic approach, consider candle magic, wherein you can dress a green or gold candle with essential oils while placing your chosen crystals around it. As you light the candle, focus on your wealth intentions, allowing the energy of the crystals to amplify your desires.

Incorporating moon phase rituals can also enhance your crystal work. During the waxing moon, focus on attracting wealth by charging your crystals under the moonlight. This practice aligns your energy with the natural cycles of abundance and growth. Affirmations and visualization techniques are crucial as well; holding your crystal while repeating wealth affirmations can help solidify your intentions. This combination of visualization and crystal energy creates a strong magnet for financial prosperity.

Clear any energy blockages that might hinder your financial success. Regularly cleanse your crystals by placing them in sunlight or moonlight, or by using sage or sound to remove negative energies. Including charms and talismans associated with abundance, alongside your crystals, can further enhance your practice. By integrating these powerful tools into your life, you can create a harmonious environment that attracts financial prosperity and supports your journey toward wealth and abundance.

Here is a list of some popularly used crystals commonly associated with prosperity and money magic:

Amazonite: Amazonite is known for its ability to promote hope and motivation, helping you attract abundance by aligning your thoughts and actions with your desires.

Aventurine: Often referred to as the "stone of opportunity," aventurine is believed to attract luck, wealth, and abundance while promoting confidence in decision-making.

Bloodstone: This crystal is thought to enhance determination and motivate you to pursue financial goals, helping you overcome obstacles.

Citrine: Known as the "merchant's stone," citrine is associated with wealth and prosperity. It is believed to enhance manifesting abilities and promote positive financial opportunities.

Clear Calcite: Clear calcite is believed to clear blockages in the flow of energy, promoting abundance and prosperity by enhancing manifesting abilities

Clear Quartz: This versatile crystal amplifies energy and intention. When focused on prosperity, clear quartz can clear mental blockages and enhance your manifesting abilities.

Emerald: Associated with growth and renewal, emerald is thought to attract financial prosperity and abundance while promoting harmony and balance in business dealings.

Garnet: Known for its energizing properties, garnet is believed to inspire motivation and ambition, helping to attract wealth and success.

Green Calcite: This crystal is thought to promote financial growth and increase abundance by encouraging the flow of energy and enhancing self-esteem.

Green Tourmaline: Associated with Earth energies, green tourmaline is believed to help with financial healing and aligning your energy with abundance.

Jade: Revered in many cultures as a symbol of prosperity, jade is believed to attract wealth, luck, and abundance.

Labradorite: This stone is believed to awaken your inner magic and protect your energy, allowing you to embrace opportunities for financial growth.

Malachite: This powerful stone is thought to absorb negative energy and promote emotional balance, encouraging positive financial growth and opportunities.

Moonstone: Known for its transformative energy, moonstone is believed to enhance intuition and attract opportunities that lead to prosperity.

Pyrite: Often called "fool's gold," pyrite is thought to promote wealth and abundance by attracting opportunities and boosting confidence.

Sodalite: This stone encourages rational thought and intuition, helping you make sound financial decisions and strategies for prosperity.

Tiger's Eye: Known for its protective properties, tiger's eye is believed to bring good luck, prosperity, and clarity of thought in financial matters.

Zebra Stone: This unique stone is an opaque chalcedony whose name alludes to its distinctive, zebra-like stripes. It is thought to promote balance and harmony when pursuing financial goals, enhancing your overall prosperity.

These crystals can be used in various ways, such as carrying them with you, placing them in your home or workspace, or using them during meditation or manifestation practices focused on abundance and prosperity.

Working with Crystals for Financial Growth

Crystals have long been revered for their energetic properties and are particularly powerful tools in the realm of financial growth and prosperity magic. For those looking to enhance their financial situation, incorporating specific crystals into your practice can amplify intention and facilitate a stronger connection to the energies of abundance. Crystals such as citrine, pyrite, and green aventurine are considered particularly beneficial for attracting wealth and prosperity. Each of these stones carries unique vibrations that can support financial intentions, and knowing how to work with them effectively is key to harnessing their potential.

To begin working with crystals for financial growth, it is essential to set clear intentions. This involves identifying specific financial goals, whether it's increasing income, finding new job opportunities, or overcoming debt. Once you have defined your intentions, choose the crystals that resonate with your goals. For example, citrine is often associated with success and confidence, making it an excellent choice for those seeking new job prospects or entrepreneurial ventures. Carrying or wearing the crystal throughout your day can serve as a constant reminder of your intentions and help to align your energy with the frequencies of abundance.

Incorporating crystals into your rituals can significantly enhance their effectiveness. One popular method is to create a prosperity jar, where you combine your chosen crystals with herbs known for attracting wealth, such as cinnamon or basil. Fill the jar with these ingredients, and as you do, visualize your financial goals manifesting. You can also use candle magic alongside your crystals; lighting a green or gold candle while focusing on your intentions can amplify the energy of the crystals. As the candle burns, hold the crystals in your hands, channeling your desires into them and visualizing your financial growth.

Utilizing moon phase rituals can deepen your work with crystals for financial prosperity. The waxing moon is an ideal time for attracting new opportunities and abundance, while the full moon is perfect for releasing financial blockages. During these phases, cleanse your crystals under moonlight, and hold them while reciting abundance affirmations or visualizing your desired financial outcomes. This practice not only aligns your energy with the natural cycles of the universe but also reinforces your intentions, making them more potent.

Consider integrating divination practices into your crystal work for financial insight. Tarot cards or pendulums can offer guidance on your financial journey, helping you identify any areas that may need attention or adjustment. Combining these tools with your crystals can create a comprehensive approach to financial growth. By consistently engaging in these practices, you will cultivate a mindset of abundance, allowing your financial goals to flourish while supporting your spiritual and magical development. Embrace the synergy of crystals and intention as you navigate your path to prosperity.

Opportunity Crystal Charm

Materials:

- A piece of citrine (for attracting success)
- A piece of clear quartz (for amplification)
- A small charm or pouch
- A piece of paper

Instructions:

1. Write down your career goals or your desired job title on the piece of paper.

2. Fold the paper and place it in the charm or pouch along with the citrine and clear quartz crystals.

3. Hold the pouch in your hands and say, "With these crystals, I attract opportunities and success."

4. Carry the pouch with you or place it on your desk as a tangible reminder of your intention to find a better job.

5. Spend a few moments each day visualizing yourself landing the job you desire while holding the pouch.

Lottery Number Crystal Ritual
Materials:
- 5 small crystals (e.g., quartz, citrine, amethyst)
- A small bowl of salt or rice
- A piece of paper and a pen
Instructions:
1. Choose crystals that resonate with luck and abundance. Cleanse them by placing them in the salt or rice for a few hours to remove any negativity.
2. Once cleansed, hold each crystal in your hand, concentrating on your intention to attract luck and specific lottery numbers.
3. Write down your chosen numbers (1-49, or the applicable range for your lottery) on the piece of paper.
4. Place the paper under the bowl of crystals. Leave it for 24 hours, allowing the energy of the crystals to charge your numbers with positive intent.
5. After the period is complete, take the paper and keep it in your wallet or a special place as a reminder of your intention for winning.

Crystal Shield for Financial Security
Materials:
- Black tourmaline or obsidian quartz (for protection)
- Green aventurine or citrine (for prosperity)
- A small bowl of water
- A few drops of lavender essential oil

Instructions:

1. Fill the bowl with water and add a few drops of lavender essential oil, which promotes peace and security.

2. Place the black tourmaline or obsidian in the water, stating, "This stone protects my financial assets."

3. Add a piece of green aventurine or citrine to the bowl, saying, "My wealth grows while safe from harm."

4. Let the bowl sit in a peaceful place for a week. Each day, focus on the stones and affirm their protective energy surrounding your finances.

5. After one week, remove the stones and place them in your home or your wallet for ongoing protection.

Creating Crystal Grids for Abundance

Creating crystal grids for abundance is a powerful practice that allows you to harness the energy of specific crystals to attract wealth and prosperity into your life. A crystal grid is a geometric arrangement of crystals, strategically placed to amplify their energy and focus it toward a specific intention—in this case, financial abundance. The beauty of this practice lies in its accessibility; anyone, regardless of their background in witchcraft or spirituality, can create a grid that resonates with their personal goals.

To start, gather crystals known for their properties related to abundance. Citrine is often referred to as the "merchant's stone" and is excellent for attracting wealth. Green aventurine is also popular for its ability to bring good luck and opportunities in financial matters. Pyrite, with its metallic luster, is another powerful crystal associated with wealth and success. Choose a few stones that you feel drawn to, as personal connection is vital in this practice. Make sure to cleanse your crystals before use, using methods such as smudging with sage or placing them under moonlight to clear any previous energies.

Once you have your crystals ready, select a quiet space where you can create your grid. A flat surface is ideal, and you may want to use a cloth that resonates with your intention—green for prosperity or gold for wealth, for example. Start by placing a central stone that embodies your main intention. This could be a larger piece of citrine or another crystal that you feel strongly about. Surround this central stone with the other crystals in a geometric pattern, such as a circle or a star. The arrangement should feel harmonious and intuitive to you, as it is essential to maintain a positive energy flow.

As you create your grid, incorporate affirmations and visualization techniques. Speak your intentions aloud, affirming your desire for financial growth and abundance. Visualize yourself achieving your financial goals, feeling the emotions associated with that success. This practice not only enhances the energy of the grid but also aligns your personal vibration with the frequency of abundance. Lighting a green or gold candle nearby can further amplify your intention and create a sacred space for your work.

After setting up your grid, spend time each day focusing on it. You can meditate in front of it, visualize your financial goals, or simply sit with the energy of your crystals. Over time, you may find that opportunities for financial growth begin to present themselves. Remember that creating crystal grids for abundance is not just about the crystals themselves; it involves a holistic approach that combines intention, energy, and action. By actively engaging with your grid, you create a powerful tool for manifesting the prosperity you seek.

Money Attraction Crystal Grid
Materials Needed:
- Green aventurine (for luck and prosperity)
- Clear quartz (for amplification)
- Pyrite (for wealth)
- A small cloth for creating the grid
- A piece of paper
Instructions:
1. On the piece of paper, write down your intentions related to attracting luck and financial opportunities.
2. Set up the cloth in a circular shape and place the crystals in a circular grid around the piece of paper.

3. As you position each crystal, visualize it amplifying your intentions: green aventurine attracting luck, clear quartz enhancing energy, and pyrite representing wealth.

4. Say, "With these stones, I open the door to prosperity and good fortune."

5. Meditate near the grid daily, focusing on the energies, and keep it displayed while you work toward your goals.

Comfortable Life Crystal Grid

Materials:

- A few crystals known for luxury and comfort (such as rose quartz, citrine, and jade)
- A small cloth or fabric to create a grid
- A piece of paper and pen

Instructions:

1. On the piece of paper, write down your desires related to comfort and luxury (e.g., financial stability, a cozy home).

2. Spread the cloth on a flat surface and arrange the crystals in a grid pattern.

3. Place the paper under one of the crystals and focus your intention on the grid, saying, "These energies align to create my comfortable life."

4. Leave the grid set up for one week while regularly visualizing your desires coming to fruition.

5. After a week, place the crystals in your living space to continue emanating that luxury energy.

Candle Magic for Financial Prosperity

Choosing the Right Candles for Money Magic

When selecting candles for money magic, it's essential to consider color symbolism, as different hues resonate with various intentions and energies. Green is the most commonly associated color with prosperity and abundance, making it an excellent choice for any financial spells. Gold, representing wealth and success, is another powerful option, often used to amplify the effects of rituals focused on attracting financial gain. For those seeking to enhance their personal power in financial matters, purple candles can be beneficial, as they are linked to spiritual and material empowerment. Additionally, white candles can serve as a versatile base for cleansing and purification, helping to remove any negative energies blocking your financial flow.

The size and shape of candles can also play a significant role in your money magic. Votive candles are ideal for focused spells, allowing for a concentrated intention over a few hours. Pillar candles, on the other hand, burn longer and can be used in more extensive rituals that require sustained energy over time. Taper candles, often used in traditional spellwork, can be employed to represent specific goals, such as paying off debt or attracting a new job. Consider the duration and type of ritual you are planning to ensure the candle you choose aligns with your intentions.

Incorporating herbs and crystals into your candle magic can enhance its effectiveness. Before lighting your chosen candle, you might want to dress it with oils infused with prosperity herbs like cinnamon or basil, which are known for their wealth-attracting properties. Additionally, placing crystals like citrine or pyrite around the candle can amplify your intentions, as these stones are renowned for their ability to attract wealth and abundance. The combination of candle energy with the vibrational frequency of these herbs and crystals creates a powerful synergy that can significantly boost your money spells.

Timing your candle magic with the lunar phases can also enhance your financial intentions. New moons are perfect for setting intentions and initiating new financial ventures, while full moons can be used for release rituals, letting go of limiting beliefs about money. Waxing moons are ideal for attracting wealth, as the energy is building, while waning moons can help in dispelling financial blockages. Aligning your candle rituals with these natural rhythms can create a more potent connection to the energies of prosperity.

Create an environment that supports your money magic. Cleanse your space using smoke from sage or incense to clear away stagnant energy, and set your intentions clearly before lighting your candle. Visualization techniques, such as envisioning the financial success you desire while focusing on the flame, can help manifest your goals. By choosing the right candles and creating a supportive ritual, you can harness the power of candle magic to invite abundance and prosperity into your life.

Candle Rituals for Attracting Wealth

Candle rituals have long been a cornerstone of prosperity magic, serving as a powerful means to attract wealth and abundance into your life. For those exploring the realms of witchcraft, particularly in the context of modern financial challenges, these rituals can be an effective way to channel intention and energy. By selecting specific colors, herbs, and crystals, practitioners can create a focused atmosphere that aligns with their desires for financial growth. For instance, green candles are traditionally associated with wealth, while gold candles symbolize success and prosperity.

To conduct a candle ritual for attracting wealth,

begin by gathering your materials. You will need a green or gold candle, some herbs known for their money-drawing properties such as basil or cinnamon, and a small dish of salt to represent purification. Before lighting the candle, create a sacred space by cleansing the area of negative energies. This can be done through smudging with sage or using crystals like black tourmaline, which is known for its grounding properties. Setting the mood with calming music or incense can further enhance the ritual experience.

Once your space is prepared, anoint the candle with oil infused with herbs that promote abundance, such as patchouli or mint. As you anoint the candle, visualize your financial goals clearly in your mind. This visualization is a crucial element of the ritual, as it sends a strong message to the universe about your intentions. When you are ready, light the candle and recite an abundance affirmation that resonates with you, such as, "I attract wealth and opportunities with ease." Repeat this affirmation as you focus on the flame, allowing yourself to feel the energy of abundance enveloping you.

During the ritual, consider incorporating additional elements like crystals, which can amplify your intention. Placing citrine or green aventurine near the candle can enhance the energy flow towards financial prosperity. You may also wish to create a prosperity jar filled with coins, herbs, and crystals, which can be placed near the candle to further draw in wealth. The jar serves as a tangible representation of your intentions and can be revisited in future rituals to refresh your commitment to financial growth.

After your candle has burned down, it is essential to close the ritual properly. Thank the energies and entities you called upon and extinguish the candle, preferably by pinching it out rather than blowing it, to preserve the energy. You may choose to keep the remnants of the candle, any herbs used, or the prosperity jar as a reminder of your intentions. Regularly revisiting this ritual, especially during auspicious moon phases or significant astrological events, can enhance your financial manifestation efforts and help clear any blockages that may impede your journey toward wealth.

Anointing and Dressing Candles for Success

Anointing and dressing candles is a powerful practice in the realm of prosperity magic, serving as a tangible way to focus your intentions and energies toward financial success. The act of dressing a candle involves applying oils, herbs, and other materials that resonate with your goals. When performing this ritual, choose a candle that correlates with your specific desires, such as green for wealth, gold for success, or white for clarity. The process allows your intentions to be infused into the candle, making it a conduit for attracting the abundance you seek.

Begin by selecting an appropriate oil to anoint your candle. Essential oils like cinnamon, patchouli, or bergamot are excellent choices for financial prosperity. These oils not only carry their own energy but also amplify your intentions. Warm the oil slightly in your hands, then rub it from the base of the candle to the wick, symbolizing drawing in wealth and success. As you anoint the candle, recite affirmations or mantras that resonate with your financial goals. This verbalization adds another layer of energy, reinforcing your desires.

Next, consider incorporating herbs into your candle dressing. Sprinkling dried herbs such as basil, mint, or chamomile onto the candle can enhance its energy. Each herb carries specific properties; for instance, basil is known for attracting wealth, while chamomile promotes prosperity and good fortune. As you sprinkle the herbs, visualize them as magnets drawing in abundance and opportunities. This step transforms the candle into a multifaceted tool that not only represents your intentions but actively participates in the manifestation process.

Once you have dressed your candle, it's essential to create a conducive environment for your ritual. Find a quiet space where you won't be disturbed and consider using crystals that resonate with financial growth, such as citrine or pyrite. Place these stones around your candle to amplify its energy. Light the candle during a moon phase that aligns with growth, such as the waxing moon, to further enhance your spell. As the candle burns, meditate on your financial goals, allowing the flame to symbolize your aspirations coming to fruition.

Finally, after the ritual, it's important to maintain the energy you've created. Keep the candle remnants in a special place, and if possible, allow the candle to burn completely. You can also create a prosperity jar, placing items that symbolize your financial goals alongside the remnants from your candle ritual. This jar acts as a continuous reminder of your intentions and provides a focal point for ongoing energy work. By regularly engaging with your prosperity magic, you cultivate a mindset of abundance that aligns with your goals, attracting the financial success you seek.

Money Protection Candle Spell
Materials Needed:
- A black candle (for protection)
- A green candle (for wealth)
- A small plate or dish
- Sea salt
- A sprig of rosemary
Instructions:
1. Place the green candle on the plate and the black candle next to it.
2. Surround the candles with a circle of sea salt, creating a protective barrier.

3. Light the green candle first, visualizing your financial abundance, then light the black candle, envisioning protection around your assets.

4. Focus on the candles for a few moments, stating, "I protect my wealth; it is safe and secure."

5. Allow the candles to burn down completely, maintaining focus on protection as they do. Dispose of the salt when done, affirming that your wealth is shielded.

Luck and Prosperity Candle Spell

Materials Needed:

- A green candle (for prosperity)
- A gold candle (for wealth and luck)
- A small plate to catch dripping wax
- A pinch of salt
- A piece of paper and pen

Instructions:

1. Write down your specific goals related to luck and prosperity on the piece of paper (e.g., "I attract wealth with ease").

2. Place the paper under the green candle and the gold candle side by side on the plate.

3. Light both candles, focusing on your intentions for prosperity and good luck.

4. Sprinkle a pinch of salt around the candles to protect your intentions, saying, "With this salt, I create a shield of protection around my wealth and luck."

5. Let the candles burn down completely, visualizing your goals becoming reality. Keep the paper in a special place to remind you of your intentions.

Herbal Sachets for Attracting Wealth

How Herbs Can Be Used to Enhance Prosperity

Herbs have long been regarded as powerful tools in the realm of prosperity magic. Their natural properties and energetic vibrations can be harnessed to attract wealth, enhance abundance, and clear financial blockages. For those seeking to incorporate herbal elements into their rituals, understanding the specific herbs associated with prosperity is essential. Popular choices such as basil, cinnamon, and mint are renowned for their ability to draw in financial stability and abundance. By integrating these herbs into your magical practices, you can elevate your intentions and create a more potent atmosphere for prosperity.

One effective way to utilize herbs for enhancing prosperity is through the creation of herbal sachets. These small pouches filled with chosen herbs can be placed in your home or carried with you to attract wealth. For instance, a sachet containing basil, chamomile, and clove can infuse your environment with uplifting energies that promote financial success. Additionally, incorporating herbal sachets into your daily routines, such as placing them under your pillow or in your workspace, can serve as a constant reminder of your financial goals, reinforcing your intentions towards abundance.

Candle magic is another powerful method to combine herbs with the energy of fire for financial prosperity. By anointing candles with essential oils derived from prosperity herbs and then rolling them in dried herbs like cinnamon or bay leaf, you can enhance your spells. Lighting a green or gold candle while visualizing your financial dreams can amplify the energies at play. The act of burning the candle serves as a release of your intentions into the universe, while the herbs provide a tangible connection to your desires for wealth and success.

Incorporating the lunar cycle into your herbal prosperity practices can also yield significant results. Each phase of the moon carries different energies that can influence your financial growth. For example, during the waxing moon, you can perform rituals using herbs like thyme and mint to attract new opportunities and abundance. Conversely, the waning moon is a perfect time to use herbs for banishing financial blockages, allowing you to make way for new wealth to enter your life. Aligning your herbal practices with the moon's phases enhances the potency of your rituals and deepens your connection to natural rhythms.

Creating a prosperity jar infused with herbs is a creative way to manifest financial goals. This jar can be filled with herbs, crystals, and personal tokens that represent your financial aspirations. As you layer the ingredients, focus on your intentions and visualize the abundance you wish to attract. Placing the jar in a prominent location serves as a continuous reminder of your goals, empowering you to take actionable steps towards achieving them. By intertwining herbs with your magical practices, you not only foster a deeper connection with nature but also create a robust framework for manifesting the financial prosperity you seek.

Herbs and Scents for Prosperity

Herbs have long been associated with prosperity and abundance in various magical traditions. Each herb carries its unique properties and energies that can be harnessed to attract wealth and financial growth. For those seeking to enhance their prosperity magic, incorporating specific herbs into rituals and spells can be a powerful way to manifest their desires. This subchapter will explore a selection of herbs commonly linked to prosperity and their magical uses, offering practical insights for modern witches and spiritual seekers.

Basil is one of the most popular herbs in

prosperity magic. Often referred to as the "money herb," basil is believed to attract wealth and good fortune. Many practitioners use basil leaves in their money spells, either by placing them in prosperity jars or incorporating them into candle magic. To enhance its effectiveness, consider carrying a basil leaf in your wallet or creating a sachet to keep in your home or workspace. The aroma of basil is also said to invite positive energies, making it a perfect addition to any abundance ritual.

Another powerful herb associated with prosperity is cinnamon. This aromatic spice is known for its ability to increase the flow of money and success. In magical practices, cinnamon is often used in the form of a powder, sprinkled on candles or added to wealth attraction spells. You can also infuse cinnamon into oils or create a cinnamon stick charm. As a warming herb, cinnamon can help ignite your passion and drive towards financial goals, making it an essential ingredient in any prosperity-focused practice.

Mint is another herb with strong associations with wealth and prosperity. Its refreshing scent is believed to bring clarity and motivation, aiding in the pursuit of financial success. Mint leaves can be used in herbal sachets, added to prosperity baths, or brewed into teas consumed during abundance rituals. The vibrant energy of mint not only attracts wealth but also helps clear away any mental blockages that may hinder your financial growth. Incorporating mint into your rituals can invigorate your intentions and enhance your overall abundance mindset.

The potent energy of chamomile makes it a valuable herb for those seeking prosperity. Chamomile is known for its calming properties, but it also carries the vibration of wealth and success. Many practitioners use chamomile in prosperity jars or as an ingredient in herbal blends for attracting abundance. The soothing energy of chamomile helps to release fear and anxiety surrounding financial matters, allowing for a more open and receptive mindset to wealth. By incorporating this gentle herb into your rituals, you can foster an environment conducive to attracting prosperity.

By integrating these herbs into your prosperity magic practices, you can enhance your ability to manifest wealth and financial abundance. Each herb not only carries its unique magical properties but also serves as a reminder of your intentions and the energies you wish to invite into your life. Whether you are a seasoned witch or a curious seeker, exploring the use of herbs in your rituals can deepen your connection to prosperity and open new pathways for financial growth.

This is a brief list of herbs commonly used for attracting money, wealth, and abundance:

Aloe Vera: Known for its protective properties, aloe vera is said to shield resources and promote prosperity, while its gel can be used in abundance rituals.

Basil: Often referred to as the "wealth herb," basil is believed to attract prosperity and success. It's commonly used in money spells and rituals.

Bay Leaves: Bay leaves symbolize success and attainment. Writing wishes or financial goals on them and burning them is a traditional way to attract prosperity.

Bergamot: Bergamot is believed to increase the flow of money and opportunities. Its essential oil is often used in prosperity spells and rituals.

Chamomile: Known for its calming properties, chamomile also attracts money and promotes general well-being. It's often used in abundance rituals to create a peaceful and receptive state.

Cedar: The scent of cedar is thought to invite abundance and prosperity. It is often used in cleansing rituals to prepare for attracting wealth.

Cinnamon: This spice is linked to prosperity and is often used in money-drawing spells. Cinnamon is believed to attract good luck and increase your financial prospects.

Cloves: Cloves are highly regarded for attracting wealth and opportunities. They can be burned or used in sachets to protect finances and draw abundance.

Dill: Dill is considered a good luck herb for attracting wealth. It's often used in cooking and magic alike to invoke prosperity.

Fennel: Fennel seeds are believed to attract wealth and luck. They are often carried in sachets or placed in prosperity rituals to encourage financial success.

Hibiscus: This vibrant flower represents wealth and attraction. Hibiscus tea is often consumed while focusing on abundance goals.

Mint: Mint is associated with abundance and growth. Its refreshing scent is thought to draw in financial opportunities and enhance wealth.

Nasturtium: This beautiful flower is associated with prosperity and courage. It can be grown in gardens as a protective herb and is used in rituals for financial growth.

Pepper: Black pepper is believed to enhance various aspects of life, including finances. It can be sprinkled in places where you desire more abundance.

Rosemary: Rosemary is commonly known for enhancing clarity and focus but is also believed to promote financial growth and stability.

Sage: Known primarily for its cleansing properties, sage can also benefit financial endeavors by clearing away negativity that might hinder prosperity.

Sweetgrass: Used in smudging, sweetgrass is said to invite positive energies that promote abundance and well-being.

Thyme: Associated with courage and protection, thyme can help ward off negative energies that may block financial success. It is sometimes included in prosperity baths.

Crafting Money Attracting Sachets

Crafting wealth attraction sachets is an enchanting practice that combines the art of witchcraft with the principles of prosperity magic. These small, magical pouches can be filled with various herbs, crystals, and symbols that amplify your intentions for financial growth and abundance. The beauty of wealth attraction sachets lies in their versatility; they can be tailored to suit your personal beliefs, preferences, and the specific energies you wish to harness. By incorporating elements such as green candles, specific herbs, and crystals, you can create a powerful tool that serves as a constant reminder of your financial goals.

To begin crafting your wealth attraction sachet, select a fabric that resonates with you. Green is often associated with prosperity, but feel free to choose any color that aligns with your energy. Once you have your fabric, gather your chosen herbs. Some popular options include basil for wealth, cinnamon for success, and chamomile for prosperity. Each herb carries its own unique properties, so consider what you want to manifest. As you fill your sachet, visualize your intentions clearly, allowing your energy to flow into the ingredients. This step is crucial, as it establishes the purpose of your sachet.

Next, consider incorporating crystals into your wealth attraction sachet. Crystals such as citrine, pyrite, and green jade are renowned for attracting abundance and fostering a mindset of prosperity. When selecting crystals, choose those that resonate with your personal energy and goals. Place the crystals in the sachet alongside the herbs, visualizing their energy combining to create a powerful force for financial manifestation. You may also wish to include affirmations or symbols that represent your financial aspirations, enhancing the potency of your sachet.

After assembling the contents, it's time to seal your sachet with intention. You can perform a simple candle magic ritual to empower your creation. Light a green candle and focus on its flame while holding your sachet. Speak your intentions aloud, affirming your desire for financial prosperity and abundance. Allow the candle to burn for a while, letting the energy infuse the sachet. Once cooled, carry the sachet with you, place it on your altar, or keep it in a special location in your home to continually attract wealth.

Maintaining a positive mindset and regularly visualizing your financial goals are essential components of this practice. Use your wealth attraction sachet as a tool for daily affirmations and visualizations. Each time you interact with it, take a moment to connect with your goals, reinforcing your belief in your ability to attract abundance. By integrating this practice into your life, you not only enhance your financial prospects but also create a deeper connection to the magic of the universe, empowering you to manifest the prosperity you desire.

Using Sachets in Daily Life

Sachets are a versatile tool in the realm of prosperity magic, serving as powerful allies in your journey toward financial abundance. These small, fabric pouches filled with herbs, crystals, and other magical ingredients can be strategically placed throughout your living space or carried with you to enhance your energy and intentions. By harnessing the properties of specific herbs and crystals known for attracting wealth, you can create sachets that resonate with your personal financial goals. Incorporating these sachets into your daily life not only amplifies your manifestation efforts but also infuses your environment with a constant reminder of your intentions for prosperity.

To create a wealth-attracting sachet, start by choosing herbs that have been traditionally associated with abundance. For example, basil is known for its ability to attract prosperity, while cinnamon can enhance your financial opportunities. Pair these herbs with crystals such as citrine or pyrite, which are often referred to as "money stones." When assembling your sachet, take the time to set your intention. As you fill the pouch, visualize your financial goals and infuse the ingredients with your energy. This act of creation not only serves to focus your intentions but also establishes a personal connection to your sachet.

Adding sachets into your daily routine can be as simple as placing them in key areas of your home or workspace. Consider placing a sachet in your wallet or purse to attract money and financial opportunities while you're out and about. You might also hang sachets in your office or workspace to enhance your productivity and draw in clients or customers. By keeping these sachets close, you continually reinforce your commitment to manifesting wealth and abundance, creating a flow of positive energy that aligns with your financial aspirations.

In addition to physical placement, you can also enhance the power of your sachets through rituals and affirmations. Lighting a green candle while focusing on your sachet can further amplify its energy. This candle magic, combined with daily affirmations about your financial situation, creates a powerful synergy that aligns your intentions with universal laws of attraction. As you repeat your affirmations, hold your sachet close, allowing its energy to merge with your words and intentions, reinforcing your belief in your ability to attract wealth.

Sachets can also serve as tools for introspection and guidance in your financial journey. Use them in conjunction with divination practices like tarot or pendulum readings, allowing the energy of the sachet to influence your insights. This approach not only provides clarity but also helps you identify any potential blockages in your financial path. By using sachets as part of your spiritual toolkit, you can cultivate a deeper understanding of your relationship with money, paving the way for a more prosperous future.

Here are four unique sachet or hex bag spells designed to attract prosperity, money, and wealth into your life. Each spell incorporates various materials and intentions to boost your financial energy.

Prosperity Herb Sachet
Materials:
- A small green or gold cloth pouch
- Dried basil (for prosperity)
- Dried mint (for attracting wealth)
- A few coins (to symbolize money)
- A small quartz crystal (to amplify energy)
- A piece of paper
Instructions:
1. Prepare Your Intentions. On the piece of paper, write down your financial goals or desires related to prosperity. Be specific about what you want to attract.
2. Fill the Sachet. In the cloth pouch, add the dried basil and mint first, followed by the coins and the

quartz crystal. As you add each item, visualize your intention manifesting.

3. Seal the Sachet. Once filled, tie the pouch securely, reciting the following affirmation:

"By herbs and coin, my wealth will grow,

Abundance surrounds me, I welcome the flow."

4. Keep or Carry It. Place the sachet in your wallet, purse, or on your altar as a constant reminder to attract prosperity into your life.

Money Attraction Hex Bag

Materials:

- A small yellow or gold fabric bag
- A piece of paper with money symbols (like the dollar sign)
- A pinch of cinnamon (for attraction)
- A green candle
- A small piece of jade or citrine (for wealth)

Instructions:

1. Write Your Intention. On the piece of paper, draw or write down symbols or affirmations that represent what you want regarding money (e.g., "Money flows easily to me").

2. Fill the Bag. In the fabric bag, add the paper, a pinch of cinnamon, and the piece of jade or citrine. As you do this, focus on the energy of abundance flowing into your life.

3. Charge the Bag. Light the green candle and hold the hex bag above the flame for a moment (carefully!) to charge it. Say:

"With this flame, I ignite my intent,
Attracting money, wealth without relent."

4. Display or Carry. Keep the hex bag on your altar, desk, or in your pocket to amplify your money attraction energies.

Abundance and Opportunity Sachet

Materials Needed:

- A small orange cloth pouch (symbolizing creativity and wealth)
- Crushed or whole cloves (for protection and prosperity)
- A small piece of paper with opportunities written on it
- A few sunflower seeds (for growth and abundance)
- A piece of paper with your name written on it

Instructions:

1. Define Your Opportunities. On the small piece of paper, write down specific opportunities or avenues for prosperity you wish to pursue (e.g., "I attract new job opportunities").

2. Fill the Sachet. In the orange pouch, add the cloves, sunflower seeds, and the paper with opportunities. Include the paper with your name, symbolizing your connection to the goal.

3. Charge Your Intentions. Hold the filled pouch in your hands and visualize the energy of growth and expansion surrounding you as you say:
  "Cloves for protection, seeds to grow,
  Opportunities flow to me, this I know."
4. Affirm and Use. Keep this sachet where you work, study, or carry it with you to enhance your capacity to attract wealth and opportunity.

Wealth Manifestation Hex Bag
Materials:
- A small black fabric bag (for protection)
- A small piece of paper
- A green candle
- A pinch of sea salt (for purification)
- A small silver coin (for prosperity)
Instructions:
1. Set Your Intent. Write down a clear statement regarding your financial goals or a specific amount of money you wish to attract.
2. Fill the Bag. Place the sea salt, paper with your intention, and the silver coin into the black bag. These items represent protection and the flow of money.
3. Light the Candle. Light the green candle and hold the hex bag above the flame (carefully!) or place it nearby. As you do this, affirm your intentions, saying:
  "Salt for protection, silver for gain,
  I call in wealth, let abundance reign."

4. Store or Carry the Bag. Keep the hex bag in your home safe, wallet, or a special place to guard and enhance your prosperity energies.

Fortune and Protection Spell Bag
Materials:
- A small green or black cloth bag
- A few coins (representing your wealth)
- A piece of green aventurine or tiger's eye crystal
- A pinch of salt
- Dried herbs (such as thyme or sage)
Instructions:
1. Fill the bag with the coins, crystal, salt, and dried herbs.
2. As you place each item into the bag, state its purpose (for example, "This coin represents my wealth; it is safe").
3. Once filled, hold the bag in your hands, saying, "I protect my fortune; it is safe wherever I go."
4. Keep this spell bag with you (in your purse or pocket) or store it in a dedicated place to maintain its protective energy around your financial assets.

Moon Phase Rituals for Financial Growth

Lunar Phases and Their Influence

Understanding lunar phases is helpful for anyone interested in prosperity magic and wealth manifestation. The moon's cycle, which lasts approximately 29.5 days, significantly influences not only the natural world but also the energies we harness for financial growth. Each phase of the moon—from the New Moon to the Full Moon and back—offers unique opportunities for different types of magic and rituals. By aligning your intentions and practices with these lunar cycles, you can enhance your ability to attract abundance and achieve financial goals.

The New Moon marks the beginning of the lunar cycle. This is a powerful time for setting intentions and planting the seeds of your desires. In the context of prosperity magic, the New Moon is ideal for initiating money spells and creating prosperity jars filled with herbs, crystals, and affirmations that align with your financial aspirations. During this phase, focus on clarity and specificity regarding what you wish to manifest. The energy of the New Moon supports new beginnings and can amplify your efforts to attract wealth.

As the moon waxes towards the Full Moon, the energy shifts to one of growth and expansion. This is the perfect time to engage in visualization techniques and abundance affirmations. The increasing light of the moon symbolizes the buildup of energy, making it an opportune moment to perform rituals involving candle magic for financial prosperity. Lighting a green or gold candle while visualizing your financial goals can help to further stimulate the energies of abundance. Additionally, this phase is great for charging crystals that attract wealth, such as citrine and pyrite, as they absorb the moon's growing energy.

When the Full Moon arrives, it is a time of culmination and realization. This phase is excellent for reflecting on what you have achieved so far and for expressing gratitude for the abundance that has come into your life. It's also a potent time for releasing any financial blockages that may be hindering your prosperity. Engaging in energy clearing practices or creating herbal sachets specifically designed for releasing negativity can be particularly effective. The Full Moon's energy can help you to let go of limiting beliefs about money, paving the way for greater financial flow.

As the moon wanes, the focus shifts to closure and letting go. This phase is valuable for divination practices that provide insights into your financial situation. Use this time for introspection, assessing your financial habits, and recognizing what may no longer serve your prosperity goals. Charms and talismans for abundance can be cleansed and recharged during this period. By understanding and working with the lunar phases, you can create a harmonious relationship between your magical practices and the natural rhythms of the universe, enhancing your journey towards financial prosperity.

Rituals for Each Moon Phase

Rituals aligned with the moon phases can greatly enhance your financial endeavors by harnessing the natural energies present at each stage. The New Moon, which symbolizes new beginnings and potential, is an ideal time for setting intentions related to wealth and prosperity. During this phase, practitioners can create a prosperity jar filled with items that resonate with their financial goals, such as coins, herbs like basil for wealth, and affirmations written on paper. As the moon waxes, focus on visualizing your financial aspirations coming to fruition. This period is perfect for money manifestation rituals, allowing you to channel your energy into attracting abundance.

As the moon transitions into the First Quarter phase, it is a time of action and growth. This is when you should actively pursue opportunities that align with your financial goals. Consider performing candle magic during this phase, using green or gold candles to symbolize growth and prosperity. Light the candle while reciting affirmations of abundance, visualizing your financial situation improving with each flicker of the flame. The energy of the First Quarter supports taking concrete steps towards your financial aspirations, whether that means applying for a new job, investing in a business, or simply reassessing your budget.

The Full Moon represents culmination and fulfillment, making it an opportune moment for gratitude and reflection. During this phase, you can perform rituals to acknowledge the abundance already present in your life. Create herbal sachets using ingredients associated with wealth, such as cinnamon and ginger, and carry them with you as talismans for attracting prosperity. Additionally, conduct a divination practice, such as tarot or pendulum readings, to gain insights into your financial path. Use this time to celebrate your achievements and release any limiting beliefs that might hinder your financial growth.

As the moon begins to wane, the Last Quarter phase encourages letting go and removing obstacles. This is a powerful time for energy clearing practices aimed at identifying and releasing financial blockages. You can create a ritual bath using herbs like rosemary for purification or perform a cleansing meditation to visualize any negative energy around your finances dissipating. This phase is also ideal for reviewing your financial strategies and making necessary adjustments. By releasing what no longer serves you, you create space for new opportunities to enter your life.

As you enter the Dark Moon, embrace this time for introspection and planning. Use this period to reflect on your financial journey, assessing what has worked and what hasn't. This phase is perfect for creating new prosperity affirmations and visualizations that will guide you into the next lunar cycle. Consider crafting charms or talismans infused with your intentions for financial growth, keeping them close as reminders of your goals. By aligning your rituals with the moon phases, you not only tap into the natural rhythms of the universe but also empower your journey toward financial abundance and prosperity.

Timing Your Financial Intentions with the Moon

Timing your financial intentions with the moon can significantly enhance your prosperity magic. The lunar cycle offers a natural rhythm that aligns beautifully with the ebb and flow of energy in the universe, making it an ideal companion for your financial goals. Each phase of the moon carries unique energies that can be harnessed to support different aspects of financial manifestation. By aligning your intentions and rituals with these phases, you can amplify your efforts to attract abundance and clear financial blockages.

The New Moon is a powerful time for setting intentions and initiating new financial ventures. This phase symbolizes new beginnings, making it the perfect moment to focus on what you want to manifest in your financial life. During the New Moon, you might create a prosperity jar filled with herbs and crystals associated with wealth. As you fill the jar, visualize your financial goals clearly and affirm your intentions, allowing the energy of the fresh lunar cycle to work in your favor. Writing down your intentions and reading them aloud can further solidify your commitment to your financial aspirations.

As the moon waxes, the energy builds, making it an ideal time for taking action on your financial plans. This phase supports growth and expansion, so it's perfect for launching projects, applying for jobs, or seeking new financial opportunities. You can enhance this period with candle magic, using green or gold candles to represent wealth. Light the candle while focusing on your goals, visualizing the growth of your financial resources. Affirmations during this time can be particularly potent, as they align your mindset with the abundance you seek.

When the Full Moon arrives, it brings a peak of energy that can be harnessed for gratitude and reflection. This phase is an excellent time to review your financial intentions and celebrate your successes, no matter how small. You might perform a ritual to release any lingering doubts or fears about your financial situation. Use herbal sachets filled with money-drawing herbs like basil or cinnamon, and place them in your space as a reminder of the abundance surrounding you. This is also a powerful time for divination practices, allowing you to gain insights into your financial path and identify any potential blockages that may need addressing.

As the moon wanes, focus on letting go of limiting beliefs and clearing space for new financial opportunities. This phase is ideal for energy clearing rituals aimed at removing financial blockages. You can create a charm or talisman infused with the intention of attracting wealth, using crystals that resonate with prosperity. As the moon decreases, visualize shedding any negative financial patterns, making room for fresh energy to flow into your financial life. By incorporating these lunar rhythms into your financial practices, you align yourself with the universe's natural cycles, enhancing your ability to manifest the wealth and abundance you desire.

New Moon Abundance Ritual

Materials:

- A piece of silver or white paper
- A silver pen
- A bowl of salt
- Essential oil (like lavender or patchouli)

Instructions:

1. During a new moon, write your financial wish or goal on the paper with the silver pen.
2. Fold the paper and anoint each corner with a drop of the essential oil.
3. Place the folded paper in a bowl of salt, saying, "From this new moon to the next, prosperity builds around me."
4. Leave the bowl in a private place, visualizing your financial wish manifesting daily.
5. At the next full moon, dispose of the salt and retain the paper in a safe place as your wealth continues to grow.

New Moon Money Manifestation Spell

Materials:

- A small piece of paper
- A pen
- A green candle (for prosperity)
- A bowl of water

Instructions:

1. On the piece of paper, write down a clear intention related to your finances (e.g., "I am open to new opportunities that bring prosperity").

2. Place the paper in front of you and light the green candle.

3. Hold the bowl of water in your hands and visualize your intention manifesting as you say, "With the new moon's energy, I call forth new paths of abundance."

4. Let the candle burn for a while while visualizing your financial goals.

5. Keep the paper in a safe place to reinforce your intention until the next new moon.

Waxing Crescent Money Attraction Spell
Materials Needed:
- A small bowl or cauldron
- Honey or sugar (to represent sweetness and abundance)
- A few coins (to symbolize money)
- A piece of green paper or cloth
Instructions:
1. Place the honey or sugar in the bowl and add the coins on top.

2. Hold the green paper or cloth, and say, "As the moon waxes, so too does my wealth grow and expand."

3. Visualize your financial abundance as you place the bowl in a visible location.

4. Each day of the waxing crescent, add a coin to the bowl to symbolize increasing wealth.

5. When the moon is full, consider what you've attracted and reflect on your money intentions.

First Quarter Moon Prosperity Spell

Materials Needed:

- A green candle
- A small dish or bowl
- A piece of parchment paper
- A pen
- Olive oil (for anointing)

Instructions:

1. Write down a specific financial goal or action you intend to take on the parchment paper (e.g., "I will apply for three jobs this week").

2. Anoint the green candle with olive oil, focusing on your goal.

3. Light the candle and place the parchment paper under it.

4. As the candle burns, say, "With the strength of the first quarter moon, I take bold steps toward my financial success."

5. Let the candle stay lit until it burns down and keep the parchment paper as a reminder of your commitment to action.

Waxing Gibbous Money Manifestation Spell

Materials:

- A small pot of soil (representing growth)
- Seeds (like basil or mint, which symbolize prosperity)
- A piece of paper and pen
- A green candle

Instructions:

1. Write down your financial intentions or goals on the piece of paper.
2. Plant the seeds in the soil while visualizing prosperity growing in your life.
3. Place the paper in the soil and light the green candle beside it.
4. Say, "As these seeds grow, so too does my financial abundance flourish."
5. Water the seeds regularly while focusing on your intentions, reinforcing the growth of your wealth.

Full Moon Water Prosperity Spell

Materials:

- A clear glass of water
- A small silver coin
- Full moon light

Instructions:

1. On the night of the full moon, place the glass of water outside or on a windowsill.
2. Drop the silver coin into the glass and let it sit under the moonlight overnight.
3. As you place the coin, say, "By the light of the full moon, my financial fortune grows."

4. In the morning, remove the coin and keep it in your wallet or pocket as a talisman for prosperity.
5. Use the water to sprinkle around your home or workspace to invite abundance.

Full Moon Abundance Ritual
Materials Needed:
- A bowl filled with rice (to symbolize abundance)
- A piece of paper
- A pen
- A gold or yellow candle
Instructions:
1. Write down three things you are grateful for regarding your current financial situation on the piece of paper.
2. Place the paper under the bowl of rice.
3. Light the gold or yellow candle and place it next to the bowl.
4. As you focus on the candle, say, "With the light of the full moon, I celebrate my abundance and attract even more."
5. Spend a few moments in meditation or reflection on gratitude and abundance, and allow the candle to burn down safely.

Full Moon Job Manifestation Ritual
Materials Needed:
- A white piece of paper
- A pen

- A small glass of water
- A silver coin
- A safe outdoor space to place items under the moonlight
Instructions:
1. On the piece of paper, write down the qualities and responsibilities of the job you want.
2. Place the silver coin on top of the paper as a symbol of wealth and success.
3. Fill the glass with water, stating, "As the moon's phases change, so do my opportunities for a better job."
4. Set the paper and water outside under the light of the full moon overnight.
5. In the morning, bring the water inside, and drink a small amount while envisioning yourself achieving your career goals. Keep the paper and coin on your altar or in a special place as a reminder of your intentions.

Waning Gibbous Letting Go Spell
Materials:
- A black or purple candle (for protection and release)
- A small bowl of water
- A piece of paper
- A pen
Instructions:

1. Write down your financial fears or limiting beliefs on the piece of paper (e.g., "I will never have enough money").
2. Light the black or purple candle and hold the paper over the flame, saying, "As this paper burns, I release my fears and limiting beliefs about money."
3. Once the paper is burned, drop it in the bowl of water. Pour the bowl outdoors someplace it will water a growing plant to reinforce the abundance energy.

Harvest Moon Wealth Ritual

Materials:
- A small bowl
- A handful of rice (representing abundance)
- A yellow or orange candle (for prosperity)
- A piece of paper and pen

Instructions:
1. During the time of the Harvest Moon, place the rice in the bowl as the base for your spell.
2. Write down your financial goals and opportunities you wish to attract on the piece of paper.
3. Place the paper underneath the bowl of rice and light the candle beside it.
4. Focus on the candle's flame and visualize the abundance as the rice symbolizes growth. Say, "As the harvest is plentiful, so will my opportunities be."
5. Let the candle burn for a while, keeping your intentions in mind. Let the rice stay in a visible place

to continually remind you of your goals and attract prosperity.

Prosperity Jars and Their Uses

What is a Prosperity Jar?

A Prosperity Jar is a powerful tool utilized in various prosperity magic practices, designed to attract wealth, abundance, and financial success into one's life. This simple yet effective ritual involves filling a jar with specific items that resonate with the energies of prosperity and abundance. Common ingredients might include coins, herbs, crystals, and personal affirmations, all strategically combined to amplify the intention behind the spell. The jar acts as a focal point for the practitioner's desires, serving as a physical representation of their goals and aspirations related to financial growth.

The creation of a Prosperity Jar begins with intention setting. Before gathering materials, it is crucial for the practitioner to reflect on their financial goals and visualize what prosperity looks like to them. This visualization can be reinforced through affirmations written on paper and included in the jar. Each item added to the jar should align with the practitioner's specific intentions; for instance, green candles can symbolize growth, while citrine crystals are often associated with wealth and success. The process of assembling the jar itself can be meditative, allowing time for the practitioner to focus on their desires and cultivate a mindset of abundance.

Once the jar is filled, it can be sealed and activated through various rituals. Many practitioners choose to utilize candle magic, lighting a green or gold candle near the jar to enhance the energy of prosperity. Some may also perform the ritual during specific moon phases, such as the New Moon, which symbolizes new beginnings and opportunities. This timing can amplify the energy of the jar and align it with the natural rhythms of the universe, enhancing its effectiveness in manifesting financial growth.

Maintaining the Prosperity Jar is just as important as its creation. Practitioners are encouraged to revisit the jar periodically, adding new items or updating affirmations as their financial circumstances evolve. This ongoing interaction with the jar keeps the energy flowing and allows for adjustments to be made as one's goals change. Additionally, some may choose to perform regular energy clearing practices to remove any financial blockages that could hinder the jar's effectiveness, ensuring that its power remains strong and focused.

Adding a Prosperity Jar into one's financial rituals not only enhances the practice of abundance but also serves as a constant reminder of the practitioner's goals. It becomes a source of inspiration and motivation, encouraging the individual to stay aligned with their vision of wealth. As part of a broader prosperity magic practice, the Prosperity Jar can be a transformative tool for those seeking to attract financial abundance into their lives, whether they are entrepreneurs, spiritual seekers, or simply individuals looking to improve their financial situation.

Ingredients for Your Prosperity Jar

When creating a prosperity jar, the choice of ingredients plays a crucial role in amplifying your intentions and attracting wealth. Begin with a base of dried herbs that are traditionally associated with abundance and financial success. Ingredients such as basil, cinnamon, and mint are powerful allies in your jar. Basil is known for its protective qualities and ability to attract wealth, while cinnamon enhances prosperity and encourages generosity. Mint not only invites money into your life but also refreshes your energy, making these herbs essential for your jar's foundation.

Crystals can significantly enhance the energy of your prosperity jar. Consider adding citrine, known as the merchant's stone, which is believed to manifest wealth and success. Pyrite, often referred to as fool's gold, is another excellent choice, symbolizing abundance and the potential for wealth. Green aventurine is also a popular crystal for attracting good fortune and prosperity. Each crystal should be cleansed before use to ensure that they resonate with your intentions and are free from any negative energy.

Including affirmations or written intentions in your prosperity jar can further focus your energy on financial growth. Write down specific goals or desires related to your financial aspirations, using positive language that reflects abundance and success. For example, phrases like "I attract wealth effortlessly" or "Opportunities for financial growth come to me easily" can serve as powerful affirmations. Place these written intentions in the jar alongside your herbs and crystals to create a concentrated source of energy that embodies your desires.

Candle magic can also be integrated into your prosperity jar ritual. Choose a green or gold candle, colors often associated with wealth and abundance. Before lighting the candle, anoint it with an oil that corresponds to your intention, such as patchouli or frankincense. As the candle burns, visualize your financial goals manifesting, allowing the flame to represent the energy you are sending out into the universe. The melting wax can also symbolize the release of any obstacles standing in the way of your prosperity.

Consider adding personal tokens or charms that hold specific meaning for you regarding wealth and success. This might include coins, small bills, or even items that symbolize your financial goals, such as a miniature house or car. These items can serve as powerful reminders of your intentions and aspirations, making your prosperity jar a deeply personal and effective tool for financial manifestation. By combining these diverse elements, you create a dynamic and potent prosperity jar that aligns with your desires, helping you to attract the financial abundance you seek.

Activating and Using Your Prosperity Jar

Activating and using your Prosperity Jar is a powerful ritual that combines intention, energy, and the universal law of attraction to manifest financial abundance in your life. The process begins with the selection of a jar that resonates with your personal energy. This could be a simple mason jar, a decorative container, or something that holds sentimental value. Once you have your jar, it's essential to cleanse it energetically. You can run it under cold water, smudge it with sage or palo santo, or leave it in the moonlight overnight. This cleansing step is crucial, as it clears any past energies and prepares the jar to attract ncw prosperity.

Next, it's time to fill your jar with items that

symbolize wealth and abundance. Common inclusions are coins, crystals like citrine or pyrite, dried herbs such as basil or cinnamon, and notes with your financial intentions written on them. Each item you add should represent your desires, whether it's a specific amount of money, a new job opportunity, or financial freedom. As you place each element into the jar, visualize your intentions clearly. Imagine the feelings of abundance, security, and success as if they are already part of your reality. This visualization is crucial because it aligns your energy with your desires, enhancing the jar's effectiveness.

Once your jar is filled, it's time to activate it. You can do this through a simple candle ritual. Choose a green or gold candle—colors that resonate with prosperity—and place it on top of your jar. As you light the candle, focus on your intentions and speak them out loud. You may also want to recite abundance affirmations or chant a money mantra that aligns with your goals. This activation process sends your energetic imprint into the universe, signaling your desire for prosperity.

After activating your jar, incorporate it into your regular prosperity practices. Keep the jar in a prominent place where you will see it daily, serving as a constant reminder of your financial goals. You may want to perform regular energy clearing around the jar using sound, crystals, or smoke to keep the energy flowing freely. Additionally, consider revisiting your jar during significant lunar phases, particularly the new moon and full moon, to set new intentions or recharge your existing ones. This ritual connection with the moon enhances the jar's power and aligns your financial goals with natural cycles.

The Prosperity Jar is not just a one-time ritual but an ongoing practice. Engage with it regularly, updating intentions or adding new items that reflect your evolving financial aspirations. You can also incorporate divination practices, such as tarot or pendulum readings, to gain insights into your financial journey. By nurturing your Prosperity Jar and maintaining a positive mindset, you activate a powerful tool for attracting wealth and abundance into your life, making it an essential part of your prosperity magic toolkit.

Opportunities Jar Spell
Materials Needed:
- A small jar with a lid
- A few pieces of paper
- A pen
- A tablespoon of sugar (symbolizing sweetness of opportunities)
- A small lucky charm (like a horseshoe or a coin)
Instructions:
1. Write down five opportunities or areas in your life where you wish to attract luck and prosperity on the

pieces of paper (e.g., "New job offer," "Investment success").

2. Fold each piece of paper and place it in the jar.

3. Add the tablespoon of sugar and the lucky charm into the jar.

4. Close the jar, holding it in your hands. Say, "This jar holds my intentions for luck and prosperity. May it attract sweet opportunities into my life."

5. Keep the jar in a special place and open it whenever you want to refocus your intentions or add more opportunities you wish to attract.

Sunrise Money Magnet Spell

Materials Needed:

- A glass jar
- A magnet
- Loose change or a small bill

Instructions:

1. At sunrise, place the magnet in the jar, along with the change or bill, as you focus on attracting financial opportunities.

2. Seal the jar and hold it up to the sun, saying, "As the sun rises, so does my wealth."

3. Store the jar in a sunny spot in your home to keep drawing money towards you.

4. Regularly add small amounts of change or bills to continuously boost the spell's energy.

Prosperity Jar Spell

Materials Needed:

- Green candle

- Small jar or container

- Coins or bills (any denomination)

- A few sprigs of basil (for prosperity)

- A piece of paper with your financial goals written on it

Instructions:

1. Light the green candle and place it in front of the jar.

2. Fill the jar with coins or bills, adding the basil as you go.

3. Fold the paper with your goals, sealing it with the jar lid.

4. Focus on your intentions for abundance as you visualize prosperity flowing into your life.

5. Allow the candle to burn out safely, and keep the jar in a prominent place to remind you of your goals.

Career Affirmation Jar

Materials Needed:

- A small jar or container

- Small slips of paper

- A pen

- Glitter (optional for visualization)

Instructions:

1. Write a series of positive affirmations related to your career success on the slips of paper (e.g., "I am a

valuable asset to my team" or "Opportunities for growth come easily to me").

2. Place the slips in the jar, adding a pinch of glitter with each affirmation to symbolize your shining potential.

3. Hold the jar in your hands and say, "With each affirmation, I attract success and fulfillment in my career."

4. Open the jar each day and read one affirmation aloud, focusing on believing and feeling the truth of each statement. Keep the jar in a prominent location to reinforce your intentions.

Luxury Manifestation Jar

Materials Needed:
- A small jar or container
- Gold glitter or gold leaf
- A piece of parchment paper
- Gold or green ribbon

Instructions:

1. On the parchment paper, write a clear intention about the luxury and comfort you wish to manifest in your life.

2. Add the gold glitter or leaf to the jar, symbolizing wealth and abundance.

3. Roll the parchment paper tightly and place it inside the jar, sealing it with the lid.

4. Tie the ribbon around the jar to finalize your intent.

5. Keep the jar visible in your space, and occasionally hold it while visualizing your dream life coming true, allowing the energy to grow over time.

Financial Shielding Salt Jar Spell

Materials Needed:

- A small jar with a lid
- Sea salt or Himalayan salt
- A few coins or small bills
- A bay leaf
- A piece of paper

Instructions:

1. Write an affirmation on the piece of paper, such as "My financial assets are secure and protected."
2. Place the coins or bills at the bottom of the jar.
3. Add the bay leaf, then pour in the salt until the jar is full.
4. As you seal the jar, repeat your affirmation, visualizing a protective barrier around your finances.
5. Keep the jar in a safe place, such as a drawer or safe, to guard your financial assets.

Divination Practices for Financial Insight

Introduction to Financial Divination

Financial divination is an ancient practice that blends the esoteric arts with the practical realm of economics and personal finance. For those who seek to enhance their financial situations through spirituality, understanding the principles of financial divination can serve as a powerful tool. This subchapter explores the significance of divination in identifying financial opportunities, clearing blockages, and manifesting prosperity through various techniques. Whether you're a seasoned practitioner or a curious newcomer, financial divination can guide your financial journey with intention and clarity.

At its core, financial divination encompasses a variety of methods that provide insight into one's financial prospects. Techniques such as tarot readings, pendulum dowsing, and rune casting allow practitioners to tap into their intuition and receive guidance regarding money matters. These methods serve not only to illuminate potential challenges but also to highlight opportunities for growth and abundance. By incorporating these practices into your financial strategy, you can gain a deeper understanding of your relationship with money and make informed decisions that align with your spiritual goals.

Witchcraft offers a plethora of tools and rituals that can enhance your financial divination practices. Crystals like citrine and pyrite are renowned for their wealth-attracting properties, while herbs such as basil and cinnamon can be used in sachets to draw in prosperity. Candle magic, too, plays a vital role; lighting candles in specific colors during financial rituals can amplify your intentions. Aligning these practices with the lunar phases can further enhance their effectiveness, allowing you to harness the natural energies of the universe for financial growth.

Affirmations and visualization techniques are also essential components of financial divination. By consistently affirming your financial goals and visualizing your desires as if they are already realized, you can shift your mindset and attract abundance into your life. This mental and emotional alignment is crucial in breaking through financial blockages and fostering a positive relationship with money. As you engage in these practices, you may find that your capacity to manifest wealth expands, revealing new paths to financial success.

Financial divination is about empowerment and transformation. By integrating these diverse practices into your life, you can cultivate an environment of abundance and prosperity. Whether through rituals, charms, or energy clearing, the goal is to create a harmonious relationship with money that reflects your values and aspirations. As you delve deeper into the art of financial divination, you may discover not only the potential for increased wealth but also a profound sense of confidence and clarity in your financial journey.

Tools for Financial Insight: Tarot, Runes, and More

In the quest for financial insight and prosperity, many modern practitioners of witchcraft and spirituality turn to ancient tools that have stood the test of time. Tarot cards, runes, and other divination methods serve as powerful conduits for understanding and manifesting wealth. These tools can help you tap into your intuition, uncover hidden opportunities, and navigate the complexities of financial decision-making. By integrating these practices into your daily routine, you can enhance your ability to attract prosperity and abundance into your life.

Tarot, with its rich symbolism and archetypes, allows for deep exploration of financial matters. Each card reveals insights about your current monetary situation, potential challenges, and opportunities for growth. For instance, drawing the Ace of Pentacles signifies new financial beginnings and opportunities, while the Five of Pentacles may indicate struggles or feelings of lack. By conducting regular tarot readings focused on your financial goals, you can gain clarity on your path and make informed decisions that align with your desires.

Runes, another ancient form of divination, offer unique perspectives on wealth and prosperity. Each rune carries specific meanings and energies that can be harnessed for financial insight. For example, the rune Fehu represents abundance and wealth, while Gebo symbolizes partnership and exchange, which can be crucial in business ventures. Creating a rune set specifically for your financial aspirations allows you to draw on their energies during rituals, enhancing your manifestation efforts. Incorporating runes into your financial practices can serve as a reminder of the potential for abundance in your life.

In addition to tarot and runes, there are various other tools and rituals that can enhance your financial insight. Crystal work is particularly potent, as certain stones like citrine and green aventurine are known for their wealth-attracting properties. Carrying these crystals or placing them on your altar during financial rituals can amplify your intentions. Similarly, candle magic, using colors associated with prosperity such as green and gold, can create a focused environment for manifesting wealth. By lighting candles while visualizing your financial goals, you can channel energy toward attracting abundance.

Using herbal sachets, prosperity jars, and moon phase rituals can further enhance your financial practices. Crafting herbal sachets filled with ingredients like cinnamon and basil can be a simple yet effective way to attract wealth. Prosperity jars, containing symbols of your financial goals, can be charged under the light of the moon to harness its energy for growth. Each of these tools serves not only as a means of divination but also as an active participant in your financial journey, helping you to clear blockages and invite abundance into your life. Embracing these practices will empower you to manifest the financial prosperity you seek.

Interpreting Financial Guidance

Interpreting financial guidance through the lens of magic and spirituality involves embracing a holistic understanding of abundance. For many, financial wisdom isn't solely about numbers; it intertwines with personal beliefs, energy, and intentions. Whether you're a Gen Z entrepreneur or a seasoned practitioner of witchcraft, recognizing that your mindset and energy can influence your financial reality is crucial. By integrating prosperity magic into your financial practices, you empower yourself to attract wealth and abundance in ways that resonate with your spiritual path.

One effective method of interpreting financial guidance is through the use of visualization techniques. By envisioning your financial goals and desires clearly, you signal to the universe your intentions. This practice can be enhanced with abundance affirmations, where you affirm your worthiness and ability to attract wealth. Combining visualization with candle magic can amplify your intentions. Lighting a green candle while focusing on your financial aspirations can create a powerful synergy that draws in prosperity. The flame not only serves as a focal point but also symbolizes the illumination of your path to financial success.

Crystals also play a significant role in interpreting financial guidance. Certain stones, like citrine and pyrite, are known for their wealth-attracting properties. Carrying these crystals or placing them in your prosperity jar can help align your energy with abundance. Additionally, creating herbal sachets filled with ingredients like basil, cinnamon, and mint can serve as a tangible reminder of your financial goals. These sachets can be placed in your workspace or under your pillow, infusing your environment with the energy of wealth and prosperity.

Harnessing the power of moon phases is another essential aspect of financial interpretation. Each phase of the moon brings unique energies that can be utilized for different financial intentions. For instance, the new moon is an ideal time for setting intentions and starting new ventures, while the full moon is perfect for releasing financial blockages. Engaging in rituals aligned with these lunar cycles can enhance your ability to attract wealth and clarity in your financial decisions, allowing you to navigate your path with confidence.

Integrating divination practices can provide valuable insights into your financial situation. Tarot cards, runes, or other divination tools can be used to uncover hidden opportunities or to reveal potential challenges. By regularly engaging in these practices, you cultivate a deeper understanding of your relationship with money, enabling you to make informed decisions that align with your spiritual beliefs. Pairing these insights with charms and talismans specifically designed for abundance can further enhance your financial journey, creating a rich tapestry of magic and practicality that guides you toward lasting prosperity.

Pendulum Prosperity Reading

Materials Needed:

- A pendulum (stone or metal)
- A green cloth or placemat
- A few coins or a small bill

Instructions:

1. Create a calm atmosphere by lighting a candle or

playing soft music.

2. Place the coins or bill in the center of the green cloth, which represents abundance.

3. Hold the pendulum over the coins and ask clear questions related to your financial situation (e.g., "Will my financial situation improve?").

4. Observe the pendulum's movements. A clockwise swing typically indicates a positive outcome, while counterclockwise may indicate challenges.

5. Record your insights in a journal, focusing on actions you can take to promote prosperity.

Tarot Money Manifestation Spread

Materials Needed:

- A tarot deck

- A pen and paper for notes

Instructions:

1. Shuffle the tarot deck while concentrating on your financial goals and desires.

2. Pull three cards and lay them out:

   - Card 1: Current financial situation

   - Card 2: What helps attract more money

   - Card 3: Potential obstacles

3. Interpret the cards and write down their meanings. Use the insights to create a plan for overcoming obstacles and enhancing prosperity.

4. Reflect on the reading once a week to stay connected with your goals and adjust your plans as needed.

Rune Casting for Abundance

Materials Needed:

- A set of runes (made of wood, stone, or any material)

- A small cloth bag

- A quiet space

Instructions:

1. Sit in a peaceful area and take a moment to center yourself, focusing on your intention for abundance.

2. While holding the rune bag, say an affirmation like, "I call on the runes to guide me in attracting abundance."

3. Draw three runes from the bag, setting them in front of you.

4. Interpret the runes regarding money and prosperity, noting how they relate to your current situation and future prospects.

5. Keep the runes close or carry one with you as a reminder of your intention.

Dice Divination for Career Success

Materials Needed:

- Two six-sided dice

- A piece of paper for notes

- A quiet space

Instructions:

1. Sit quietly and concentrate on your professional goals before rolling the dice.

2. Roll the two dice and add the numbers together to get a total.

3. Refer to a predetermined list assigning each total (2-12) a specific meaning or insight related to career and prosperity (e.g., 2 might indicate new beginnings, while 7 could suggest a time of reflection and planning).

4. Write down the meaning and any actionable steps you can take toward enhancing your career prosperity.

5. Repeat this ritual weekly to track changes or progress based on your rolling results.

Scrying for Financial Clarity

Materials:

- A shallow bowl of water or a clear crystal ball
- A candle (preferably green or gold)
- A comfortable space with low lighting

Instructions:

1. Fill the bowl with water and place it in front of you, lighting the candle nearby to cast soft reflections.

2. Take a few deep breaths and focus on your financial goals and questions.

3. Gaze into the water or crystal ball, allowing your mind to relax. Watch for shapes, reflections, or messages that may surface.

4. Pay attention to any images or feelings that arise, interpreting them as signs or insights related to

money and prosperity.

5. Journal your impressions and plan any steps based on the visions you received.

Charms and Talismans for Abundance

Types of Charms and Talismans for Wealth

Charms and talismans have long been utilized across various cultures as tools to attract wealth and abundance. For modern practitioners of prosperity magic, these enchanted objects can serve as powerful aids in manifesting financial success and overcoming economic challenges. Understanding the different types of charms and talismans designed for wealth can empower individuals to create a personalized approach to their financial aspirations. Each type carries unique symbolism and energy, making it important to choose those that resonate with one's specific intentions.

One popular category of wealth charms includes crystals known for their financial properties. Crystals such as citrine, pyrite, and green aventurine are often sought after for their ability to attract prosperity and amplify positive energy. Practitioners can carry these stones in their pockets, place them on their workspaces, or incorporate them into wealth manifestation rituals. The vibrational qualities of these crystals can help clear financial blockages and align one's energy with abundance, providing a tangible connection to one's goals.

Herbal sachets also serve as effective talismans for wealth attraction. By combining herbs traditionally associated with prosperity, such as basil, cinnamon, and chamomile, individuals can create powerful sachets that can be kept in homes, businesses, or carried on their person. These sachets can be infused with specific intentions through visualization and affirmations, transforming them into potent tools for manifesting financial growth. Additionally, the use of herbs connects practitioners to nature, enhancing their spells with natural energies.

Candle magic is another method that can be seamlessly integrated into wealth attraction practices. Different colored candles, particularly green for prosperity and gold for success, can be used in ritualistic settings to enhance one's financial intentions. Lighting a candle while focusing on abundance affirmations or visualizing financial goals can create a powerful energetic shift. The flames symbolize transformation, allowing practitioners to release old financial patterns and invite new opportunities into their lives.

Prosperity jars stand out as a creative and interactive way to manifest wealth. These jars can be filled with items that symbolize abundance, such as coins, grains, or herbs, and can be charged with specific intentions. By keeping the jar in a prominent place, individuals are continually reminded of their financial goals, reinforcing their commitment to abundance. Such tangible representations of prosperity not only serve as focal points for energy but also as daily reminders of the potential for financial growth and success.

Creating Your Own Prosperity Talismans

Creating your own talismans for abundance is a powerful practice that allows you to harness the energy of intention and manifestation tailored specifically to your financial goals. Talismans serve as physical representations of your desires, inviting in the energy of prosperity and wealth. To begin, select materials that resonate with you personally. This could include crystals known for their abundance properties, such as citrine or green aventurine, or natural items like herbs and oils that align with your intention. The act of choosing these materials is a crucial step, as it sets the stage for your connection to the talisman.

Once you have your materials, it is essential to cleanse them of any prior energy they may carry. This can be achieved through various methods, such as smudging with sage or placing them under the light of the full moon. Cleansing not only prepares your materials for use but also enhances their ability to attract financial prosperity. After cleansing, you can charge your talisman with your intention. This is where visualization plays a key role. Envision your financial goals clearly and feel the emotions associated with achieving them as you hold your chosen materials. This energetic alignment amplifies the effectiveness of your talisman.

Adding candle magic into your talisman creation can deepen the ritual. Choose a candle color that corresponds to abundance—green or gold are popular choices. As you light the candle, focus on your intentions and visualize the flame as a beacon of prosperity drawing wealth towards you. Allow the candle to burn down completely if possible, as this symbolizes the release of your intentions into the universe. Alternatively, you can carve symbols or words related to abundance into the candle before lighting it, further infusing it with your desires.

After the candle ritual, place your talisman in a dedicated space within your home or carry it with you to keep your intentions active. Regularly interacting with your talisman, whether through meditation or speaking abundance affirmations, helps maintain its energetic charge. You might consider creating a prosperity jar alongside your talisman, filled with items that represent wealth and abundance, such as coins, herbs, and written affirmations. Combining these practices can create a synergistic effect, enhancing your overall manifestation efforts.

Abundance talismans are not just about the physical object; they also serve as reminders of your intentions and goals. Regular reflection on your financial aspirations and progress can help you stay aligned with the energy of abundance. Use divination practices to check in on your financial journey and adjust your rituals as needed. By embracing the creative process of making your own abundance talismans, you not only engage with the magic of wealth attraction but also empower yourself to shape your financial destiny.

Carrying and Charging Your Abundance Charm

Carrying and charging your abundance charm is a vital practice in the realm of prosperity magic, serving as a personal conduit for attracting wealth and success into your life. To begin with, selecting the right charm is crucial. This could be a crystal, a talisman, or even a small pouch filled with herbs associated with abundance, such as cinnamon or basil. Each item carries its unique energy and properties, so choose one that resonates with your intentions. As you hold your charm, visualize it filled with your desires, amplifying its power to attract financial prosperity.

Once you have your charm, the next step is to charge it effectively. This can be done through various methods, including moon phase rituals, which align your charm with the natural cycles of abundance and growth. For instance, charging your charm during a waxing moon invites new opportunities, while a full moon can amplify its energy. You can also incorporate candle magic by lighting a green candle, which symbolizes wealth, and placing your charm nearby. As the candle burns, focus on your intentions, visualizing the flow of abundance entering your life.

Carrying your abundance charm daily is essential to maintain its energy. Keep it in your pocket, purse, or as part of your daily attire, ensuring it remains close to you. The more you interact with your charm, the more energy it absorbs from your intentions and the surrounding environment. Consider creating a simple affirmation to recite whenever you touch or see your charm, reinforcing your commitment to attracting prosperity. This practice helps to keep your mindset aligned with abundance, inviting more opportunities into your life.

In addition to daily carry, it's important to periodically cleanse and recharge your charm to clear any stagnant energy. This can be done through various methods, such as smudging with sage or placing the charm in a bowl of salt. Depending on its material, you might also use water or sunlight for cleansing purposes. After cleansing, repeat the charging process, infusing the charm with fresh intentions and energy, ensuring it remains a powerful tool for manifesting wealth.

Document your experiences with the charm. Keep a journal detailing the moments when you feel its energy most strongly, or when you notice financial opportunities arising. This practice not only helps you track your progress but also reinforces the connection between your charm and your financial growth. By nurturing this relationship, you empower your charm to serve as a constant reminder of your abundance mindset, enhancing your overall prosperity journey.

Lucky Charm Creation

Materials Needed:

- A small stone or crystal (e.g., citrine for abundance)
- Gold or green paint
- A small paintbrush
- A personal touch (like initials or a special symbol)

Instructions:

1. Hold the stone or crystal in your hands, closing your eyes and focusing on your desires for luck and prosperity.
2. Using the paint, create symbols or write messages that resonate with your intentions.
3. Allow the charm to dry, then keep it in your wallet, purse, or workplace to attract positive energy and luck.

Lucky Coin Talisman Spell

Materials:

- A shiny coin (preferably one that holds personal significance)
- Green or gold fabric (for wrapping)
- A small bowl of salt
- A candle (green or gold)
- A piece of paper and a pen

Instructions:

1. Set Your Intention: Sit in a quiet space and hold the coin in your hands. Close your eyes and focus on what you want this talisman to bring you (e.g., luck, success, abundance). Visualize your intention clearly.

2. Charge the Coin. Light the candle and sprinkle a pinch of salt around the candle. This adds protective energy. Hold the coin above the flame (without touching it) while repeating the following affirmation three times:

"With this coin, luck I will find,

Prosperity flows, and blessings unwind."

3. Wrap the Coin: After charging the coin, wrap it in the green or gold fabric. As you wrap, continue to visualize and affirm your intention, knowing that the coin now holds the energy of your desires.

4. Create a Power Spot. Find a safe place to keep your wrapped coin (e.g., your wallet, a special box, or your altar). This charm will now serve as a reminder of your intention, attracting positive energies and opportunities.

Crystal Luck Charm Spell

Materials:

- A small crystal or stone (e.g., citrine for prosperity, aventurine for luck)
- A clear piece of paper or parchment
- A pen
- A small pouch (made of fabric or leather)
- A pinch of dried herbs (such as basil or mint)

Instructions:

1. **Set Your Intention:** Write down your specific intention for luck on the piece of paper. Be clear and concise about what you hope to attract or achieve.

2. Charge the Crystal. Hold the crystal in your dominant hand and visualize it glowing with light. As you focus, say the following incantation:

"This crystal shines, luck it brings,

Fortune flows as joy it sings."

3. Gather Your Materials. Place the written intention and a pinch of the dried herbs into the small pouch, along with the charged crystal. The herbs will enhance the charm's energy and potency.

4. Seal the Charm. Tie the pouch closed securely, visualizing the energy of your intention being sealed inside. Carry this pouch with you at all times or place it on your altar. Whenever you touch it or see it, remind yourself of your goal to attract good luck and prosperity.

Prosperity Magic for Specific Needs

Debt Relief Spells

Debt relief spells offer a unique approach to addressing financial burdens by harnessing the power of intention, ritual, and energy work. For many Americans facing the pressures of student loans, credit card debt, or unexpected expenses, these spells can serve as a spiritual tool to clear financial blockages and invite abundance into one's life. By focusing on specific techniques that resonate with various spiritual practices, practitioners can create targeted spells aimed at alleviating their financial stress and promoting a healthier relationship with money.

One effective method is the use of candle magic. Selecting green or gold candles, which symbolize wealth and prosperity, practitioners can carve symbols or words representing their intentions for financial relief. Lighting the candle during specific moon phases, especially during the waxing moon, can amplify the energy of growth and attraction. As the candle burns, it serves as a focal point for visualization, allowing individuals to imagine their debts being reduced and their financial situation improving. This practice not only enhances the spell but also reinforces a mindset conducive to attracting prosperity.

Incorporating crystals into your debt relief spells can significantly enhance their effectiveness. Crystals such as citrine, pyrite, and green aventurine are known for their wealth-attracting properties. Creating a crystal grid dedicated to financial relief can harmonize energies and invite abundance into your life. Place these crystals in a small pouch or alongside your prosperity jar, which can be filled with herbs, coins, and symbols of your financial goals. Each time you engage with your crystals, you strengthen your intention and keep your focus on manifesting financial freedom.

Herbal sachets also play an important role in debt relief spells. By combining herbs like basil, cinnamon, and chamomile, which are known for their money-drawing properties, practitioners can create sachets that attract wealth and provide protection against financial loss. Placing these sachets in your wallet, under your pillow, or near your workspace can serve as a daily reminder of your intentions and keep the energy of abundance flowing. Additionally, using affirmations that align with your financial goals while carrying these sachets can further reinforce your commitment to manifesting prosperity.

Integrating divination practices can provide insight into your financial situation and guide your spellwork. Tarot cards, runes, or pendulums can help clarify the steps you need to take to alleviate your debt. Using these tools in conjunction with your spells can create a comprehensive approach to financial relief. By understanding the energies at play in your financial life, you can tailor your spells to address specific issues, leading to a more harmonious and prosperous existence. Embracing these practices not only aids in reducing financial burdens but also empowers individuals on their journey toward wealth and abundance.

Clearing Debt Release Spell

Materials:

- A piece of paper
- A pen
- A small bowl of water
- A candle (white or green)
- A pinch of salt

Instructions:

1. Write It Down. On the piece of paper, write down the total amount of your debt or the specific debts you wish to release. Be clear about the amounts and any feelings you have associated with them.

2. Create a Sacred Space. Light the candle and place it

nearby. This will represent your intention to illuminate the path toward financial freedom.

3. Release and Purify. Sprinkle a pinch of salt in the bowl of water, symbolizing purification and clarity. Hold the paper over the bowl and express your intentions for debt relief out loud. Say a release affirmation, such as:

"With this water, I cleanse my debts,

I pave the way for freedom's debts.

Let burdens lift and worries cease,

Abundance flows, and I find peace."

4. Dissolve the Paper. Carefully dip the paper into the water, allowing it to absorb the water and dissolve (if using regular paper, you can tear it into smaller pieces as it absorbs). Dispose of the remnants outside or in a safe place, symbolizing the release of your debt.

5. Close the Ritual. Allow the candle to burn out safely, signifying the end of the spell and your commitment to taking steps toward financial wellness.

Abundance Flow Spell

Materials:

- A small green or gold cloth pouch
- A few coins or bills (any denomination)
- A piece of paper and a pen
- Cinnamon or a few grains of sugar (for attracting abundance)

Instructions:

1. Prepare Your Intention. On the piece of paper, write positive affirmations related to your financial goals (e.g., "I am attracting abundance and releasing all fear related to debt."). Make it uplifting and aspirational.

2. Fill the Pouch. Place your affirmations into the green or gold pouch, followed by the coins or bills and a pinch of cinnamon or sugar. These ingredients will symbolize fertility and abundance.

3. Focus on Your Intent. Hold the pouch in your hands and visualize the flow of money and abundance coming into your life while simultaneously feeling any worries about debt dissipate. Say the following affirmation:

"Money flows, problems cease,

Abundance surrounds and gives me peace.

I release my debt and welcome ease."

4. Keep the Charm Close. Carry the pouch with you or place it in a prominent location in your home or workspace as a reminder of your commitment to creating positive financial energy.

Debt Acknowledgment and Release Spell

Materials Needed:

- A black or dark candle
- A piece of paper
- A lighter or matches
- A bowl for ashes (fireproof)

- A small mirror

Instructions:

1. Acknowledge Your Situation. On the piece of paper, write down the debts you wish to acknowledge, allowing yourself to express any fears or emotions tied to them. This is a moment of honesty and acceptance.

2. Light the Candle. As you light the black candle, think of it as a way to absorb negativity related to your financial situation.

3. Burn Your Worries: Hold the paper over the flame of the candle (carefully!) and let it burn, allowing the ashes to fall into the bowl. As it burns, say:

"I acknowledge and accept my debt,

Let this flame erase all regret.

I release this burden, let it be done,

I welcome abundance; I'm ready for fun."

4. Reflect in the Mirror. Once the paper has completely burned, hold the mirror in front of you, gaze into it, and visualize a future free from debt. Affirm your commitment to making mindful choices to create abundance.

5. Close the Ritual. Once complete, extinguish the candle safely and dispose of the ashes outside, symbolizing your release of the debt.

Protection from Debt Collectors Spell

Materials:

- A black candle (for protection)

- A white candle (for clarity and peace)
- A piece of paper
- A pen
- A small bowl of salt
- A fireproof container for burning

Instructions:

1. Set Up Your Altar. Find a quiet space where you can focus. Place the black candle on the left side and the white candle on the right side. In front of them, place the bowl of salt.

2. Write Your Intention. On the piece of paper, write a statement affirming your intention to avoid communications from debt collectors. For example: "I am protected from all unwanted communications regarding my debts."

3. Light the Candles. Light the black candle first, visualizing it absorbing all negativity and threats related to debt collectors. Then, light the white candle, envisioning it bringing clarity and peaceful energy into your life.

4. Empower with Salt. Sprinkle a circle of salt around the candles and the paper, forming a protective boundary. As you do this, say:

"With this salt, I create a barrier,

To shield me from calls that cause me to falter.

I stand strong, my spirit intact,

No debt collector shall invade this pact."

5. Burn the Paper. Carefully burn the paper in the flame of the white candle, letting the smoke carry

your intention into the universe. Once it's burnt, place the ashes in the fireproof container.

6. Close the Ritual. Let the candles burn for as long as possible. When you feel comfortable, extinguish them safely. Dispose of the ashes and salt in nature or a safe place, symbolizing the release of your intention.

Silencing Debt Collector Calls Spell

Materials:

- A piece of black thread or string

- A small piece of black fabric (like a pouch)

- A few drops of lavender or calming essential oil

- A small piece of paper

- A pen

Instructions:

1. Prepare the Pouch. Take the small piece of black fabric and form it into a pouch by tying it with the black thread. This will serve as your protective charm.

2. Write Down Your Intention. On the piece of paper, write a clear declaration of your desire to silence debt collector calls, such as: "I call upon the universe to guard me against unwanted communications regarding my debts."

3. Anoint the Pouch. Place a few drops of lavender essential oil on the fabric pouch. Lavender is known for its calming properties, which will help create a peaceful environment.

4. Fill the Pouch. Fold the paper with your intention

and place it inside the pouch along with the string. As you do this, visualize a barrier forming around you, preventing debt collectors from reaching you.

5. Manifest the Protection. Tie the pouch closed while saying:

"Threads of black, silence each call,

Protect my spirit; let peace fill my hall.

No debt collector shall breach this bind,

In this charm, my peace I find."

6. Keep the Charm Accessible. Carry the pouch with you in your bag or keep it somewhere close in your living space, such as your nightstand or wallet. Whenever you feel anxious about receiving calls, hold the pouch and reaffirm your intention for peace and protection.

Career Advancement Rituals

In the pursuit of career advancement, many individuals seek methods that blend traditional wisdom with modern practices. Rituals designed to attract promotions and recognition can be powerful tools for those who wish to elevate their professional lives. These practices often incorporate elements of prosperity magic, utilizing various techniques to align intentions with the forces of abundance. By understanding and integrating these rituals into daily life, practitioners can create a more conducive environment for their career aspirations.

One of the most effective tools for enhancing

career prospects is the use of crystals. Crystals like citrine and pyrite are renowned for their ability to attract wealth and success. To harness their energy, simply carry these stones during interviews or important meetings, or place them on your workspace. Additionally, creating a crystal grid specifically for career advancement can amplify your intentions. Position the stones in a geometric pattern that resonates with your goals, allowing their energies to harmonize and draw in the recognition you seek.

Candle magic is another powerful ritual that can be employed to manifest career growth. Choose a green or gold candle, colors associated with prosperity and success. As you light the candle, visualize your ideal job promotion or recognition vividly. Speak your intentions aloud, affirming that you are deserving of success. Allow the candle to burn down completely, focusing on your goals with each flicker of the flame. This act not only symbolizes your commitment but also sends a clear message to the universe about your desires.

Incorporating herbal sachets into your routine can further enhance your efforts. Create a sachet using herbs such as basil, cinnamon, and bay leaves, each known for their wealth-attracting properties. Carry the sachet with you or place it in your workspace to invite abundance. Additionally, consider performing a ritual during the new moon, a time for new beginnings and intentions. Write down your career goals, fold the paper, and place it in your sachet, infusing it with the energy of your aspirations.

Energy clearing practices can help remove any blockages that may hinder your professional growth. Regularly smudging your space with sage or using sound healing techniques can purify your environment, making it more receptive to your desires. Additionally, employing divination practices, such as tarot or runes, can provide insights into your career path, guiding you toward opportunities for advancement. By integrating these rituals into your life, you create a holistic approach to career development that honors both your spiritual journey and professional aspirations.

Career Path Visualization
Materials Needed:
- A blank piece of paper
- Colored pens/pencils
- A quiet space for meditation
Instructions:
1. Find a comfortable, quiet place and take a few deep breaths to center yourself.
2. Close your eyes and visualize your ideal career scenario – imagine yourself thriving in that role.
3. Once you have a clear image, open your eyes and draw or write about this vision on the paper.
4. Place the paper in a place where you will see it often, reinforcing your visualization daily.

Vision Board for Career Success
Materials Needed:
- A large poster board or cork board
- Magazines or printouts of your dream job and career milestones
- Scissors
- Glue or pins
Instructions:
1. Cut out images, words, and phrases that resonate with your career aspirations and success.
2. Arrange them on the board in a visually pleasing way, ensuring it reflects your goals and aspirations.
3. As you glue down each item, recite affirmations related to each image (e.g., "This is my ideal work environment," or "I am capable of achieving this success").
4. Place the vision board in your workspace or another prominent area to serve as a daily reminder of your career goals.
5. Spend time each day looking at the board, visualizing your journey toward success and the steps you'll take to achieve it.

Career Growth Crystal Grid
Materials:
- A small piece of clear quartz (for amplification)
- A piece of citrine (for prosperity)
- A piece of tiger's eye (for focus and determination)

- A small cloth for the grid

Instructions:

1. On the cloth, arrange the crystals in a triangle or other pleasing geometric shape.

2. Place a small sheet of paper in the center with your career goals written on it.

3. As you arrange the crystals, visualize each one enhancing different aspects of your professional life: clear quartz amplifying energy, citrine attracting prosperity, and tiger's eye providing focus.

4. Say a mantra such as, "These energies unite to guide my path to success."

5. Leave the grid undisturbed for several days, and meditate on it daily to reinforce your career intentions.

Job Search Candle Spell

Materials Needed:

- A blue candle (for communication and clarity)
- A green candle (for prosperity)
- A piece of paper
- A pen
- A small bowl of water

Instructions:

1. Write your ideal job description on the paper, detailing what you seek in a new position.

2. Place the paper under the blue candle and light both the blue and green candles.

3. As you light the candles, visualize yourself in the job you desire, feeling confident and fulfilled.

4. Dip your fingers into the bowl of water and sprinkle a few drops over the candles, stating, "With this water, I cleanse any obstacles in my path to finding my ideal job."

5. Allow the candles to burn completely, focusing on your intentions. When done, keep the paper in a safe place as a reminder of your goals.

Job Finding Vision Board

Materials Needed:

- A large poster board or cork board
- Magazines or images representing your dream job
- Scissors
- Glue or pins
- Markers

Instructions:

1. Cut out images, words, and phrases from magazines that resonate with your ideal job and career goals.

2. Arrange these cutouts on the board to create a vision of your desired work life.

3. As you glue or pin each item, say affirmations such as, "I am attracting my ideal job with ease" or "Opportunities come to me."

4. Place the vision board in a visible area, such as your room or workspace, as a daily reminder of your career aspirations.

5. Spend a few moments each day reflecting on the board and visualizing yourself in the desired job role.

Job Hunt Protection and Clarity Spell
Materials:
- A small bowl of rice or salt (to symbolize abundance)
- A white candle (for purity and new beginnings)
- A piece of paper
- A pen
Instructions:
1. On the piece of paper, write down your intentions for clarity and protection during your job search (e.g., "I attract only the best opportunities for me").
2. Light the white candle and place it in front of the bowl of rice or salt.
3. Hold the paper over the flame, saying, "I release any doubts or negativity holding me back. I am open to new job opportunities."
4. Place the paper beside the bowl and visualize a clear path to your ideal job, free from distractions.
5. Allow the candle to burn down safely, while the rice or salt continues to represent abundance and protection in your job search.

Job Interview Confidence Spell
Materials Needed:
- A small mirror
- A white candle (for purity and clarity)

- A bay leaf
- A small bowl of water
Instructions:
1. Light the white candle and place it in front of the mirror.
2. Hold the bay leaf and look into the mirror, stating, "I reflect confidence and competence in all my interviews."
3. After a moment, write your name on the bay leaf and place it in the bowl of water, stating, "This water cleanses me of doubt and prepares me for success."
4. Visualize your successful interview experience while the candle burns. Allow the candle to extinguish naturally, and keep the leaf and water nearby until your interview.

Business Success Spells

Business success spells are practical techniques that align spiritual practices with entrepreneurial ambitions, creating a unique blend of magic and strategy for enhancing business prospects. These methods, rooted in various traditions of witchcraft and prosperity magic, empower practitioners to attract wealth and manifest abundance in their professional lives. By incorporating these spells into daily routines, individuals can clear energetic blockages, foster positive intentions, and cultivate an environment that is conducive to success.

One effective technique for enhancing business

prospects is the use of candle magic. By selecting specific colors associated with prosperity—such as green for abundance or gold for wealth—entrepreneurs can focus their intentions during rituals. Lighting candles while visualizing their business goals can amplify the energy directed toward achieving those aspirations. Pairing this practice with affirmations that reinforce a mindset of success further enhances its effectiveness. For example, repeating phrases like "I attract profitable opportunities" can shift one's energy and mindset, making it easier to recognize and seize chances for growth.

Another powerful approach is the creation of prosperity jars. These jars serve as focal points for intentions and can be filled with items that symbolize wealth, such as coins, herbs like cinnamon and basil, and crystals like citrine or pyrite. The process of assembling a prosperity jar can itself be a ritual, allowing practitioners to imbue the jar with their desires. Placing the jar in a prominent location serves as a daily reminder of one's goals and can attract positive energy and opportunities for financial growth.

Energy clearing practices are also essential for removing financial blockages that may hinder success. Techniques such as smudging with sage or using sound healing, like singing bowls, can help cleanse the space of negative energy. Following this, divination practices such as tarot readings or pendulum work can provide insight into financial decisions and opportunities. These tools not only offer guidance but also help in aligning one's energy with the universe's flow, making it easier to attract wealth and prosperity.

Utilizing the phases of the moon can amplify business success spells. Each lunar phase offers unique energies that can be harnessed for different aspects of financial growth. For instance, the new moon is ideal for setting intentions and starting new ventures, while the full moon can be a time for gratitude and abundance recognition. By aligning business goals with these natural cycles, practitioners can maximize their manifestation efforts, creating a rhythm that supports sustained prosperity. Incorporating these techniques into everyday business practices can create a powerful synergy between magic and entrepreneurship.

Success Candle Spell
Materials:
- A yellow candle (for success and motivation)
- A green candle (for prosperity)
- A piece of paper
- A pen
- Cinnamon powder
Instructions:

1. Write your career goals on the piece of paper in present tense, as if they have already been achieved (e.g., "I am thriving in my dream job").
2. Place the paper under the yellow candle, which represents your success.
3. Light both candles while focusing on your goals, visualizing success flowing into your professional life.
4. Sprinkle a small amount of cinnamon powder around the candles, stating, "With this spice, I attract opportunity and wealth."
5. Let the candles burn while concentrating on your intentions. Repeat your goals aloud, reinforcing your desire for career success, and allow them to burn safely.

Success Empowerment Spell

Materials Needed:

- A green or yellow candle (representing success and positivity)
- A small piece of paper
- A pen
- A clear container (like a glass or a bowl)
- A small amount of dirt or sand (optional)

Instructions:

1. Prepare Your Space. Find a quiet area where you won't be disturbed. Light the green or yellow candle, symbolizing your goal of success.
2. Set Your Intention. On the piece of paper, write the specific task you want to succeed at. Be clear and

precise. For example, "I will successfully complete my project presentation."

3. Empower the Paper. Hold the paper in your hands and visualize yourself completing the task with confidence and ease. Imagine the feelings of accomplishment and satisfaction.

4. Seal Your Intention. Place the paper into the clear container. If you wish, you can add a little dirt or sand to symbolize the grounding of your intention. As you do this, say aloud:

"Rooted and grounded, I focus my mind,
Success in my task is what I shall find.
With this flame, my purpose ignites,
I succeed as I strive, guided by light."

5. Allow the Candle to Burn. Let the candle burn for a while as you continue to visualize your success. If needed, you can extinguish it and relight it later until it burns out completely. Keep the paper in the container as a reminder of your intention.

Motivation and Focus Spell

Materials Needed:

- A piece of blue or purple cloth (for clarity and focus)

- A small, clear quartz crystal (for amplified energy)

- A small bowl of water

- A piece of paper

- A pen

Instructions:

1. Create Your Workspace. Lay the blue or purple cloth on a flat surface to create a sacred space for your spell.

2. Write Down Your Goals. On the piece of paper, write a succinct statement that reflects your desired outcome. For instance, "I am focused and motivated to achieve [specific task]."

3. Focus with Water. Place the bowl of water next to the cloth. Water symbolizes clarity and can help refresh your mind. As you place the bowl down, say:

"Water of clarity, guide my thoughts,

Focus my mind, let distractions be thoughts."

4. Charge the Crystal. Hold the clear quartz crystal in your hands and say:

"With this crystal, I harness my might,

Clarity and focus flow within me tonight."

5. Combine the Elements. Place the piece of paper under the crystal and the bowl of water on top of it. Visualize the energy of focus and motivation flowing through the crystal and into your task.

6. Hold the Intention. Take a moment to meditate on your goal, feeling the sense of accomplishment that comes with it. You can keep the cloth, crystal, and water setup for a few days as you work on your task, continually visualizing your success.

Energy Clearing for Financial Blockages

Identifying Financial Blockages

Identifying financial blockages is a crucial step in your journey toward prosperity. These blockages can manifest as limiting beliefs, emotional traumas, or even external circumstances that hinder your financial growth. Acknowledging these barriers is essential for anyone seeking to harness the power of prosperity magic effectively. Begin by examining your mindset around money. Often, our upbringing and societal conditioning shape our financial beliefs, leading to feelings of unworthiness or fear associated with wealth. By recognizing these mental patterns, you can start to dismantle them through affirmations and visualization techniques that reinforce your ability to attract abundance.

Emotional blockages also play a significant role in your financial landscape. Past experiences, such as financial struggles or feelings of inadequacy, can create an energetic residue that affects how you perceive and interact with wealth. Engaging in energy clearing practices, such as meditation or smudging, can help release these old energies. Additionally, financial blockages can be tied to specific emotional states like anxiety or guilt surrounding money. Acknowledging these emotions allows you to address them head-on, paving the way for a healthier relationship with your finances.

Consider also the external factors that may contribute to financial blockages. These can include toxic relationships, unsupportive environments, or even societal pressures that discourage financial ambition. Surrounding yourself with a supportive community, whether through spiritual groups or networking with like-minded entrepreneurs, can help mitigate these influences. Cultivating a positive network creates an environment that fosters abundance. You may also find it beneficial to create a prosperity jar or utilize wealth-attracting crystals as physical representations of your intention to overcome these external barriers.

The moon phases play a significant role in identifying and releasing blockages. Each phase offers unique energy conducive to specific intentions. For example, the new moon is an ideal time for setting financial intentions, while the full moon is perfect for releasing what no longer serves you. Incorporating moon phase rituals into your financial practices can enhance your awareness of blockages and provide a structured approach to addressing them. Keeping a journal to document your feelings and observations during these rituals can deepen your insights and help track your progress over time.

Divination practices can be invaluable tools for uncovering hidden financial blockages. Tarot, pendulums, or runes can offer insights into areas of your life where you may be unconsciously sabotaging your financial well-being. By regularly engaging in these practices, you can gain clarity and direction, empowering you to take actionable steps toward overcoming obstacles. Remember, identifying financial blockages is not just about recognizing what holds you back; it is also about celebrating the progress you make in releasing those barriers on your path to prosperity.

Mindset Clearing Ritual

Materials:

- A mirror
- A notebook and pen
- A comfortable space

Instructions:

1. Prepare Your Space. Find a quiet, comfortable area where you can focus without distractions. Sit in front of a mirror where you can see your reflection.

2. Self-Reflection. Take a few deep breaths and center yourself. Look into the mirror and ask yourself, "What limiting beliefs do I hold about money?"

Allow any feelings or thoughts to arise. Write them down in your notebook as they come to you.

3. Affirmation Creation. Once you have identified these limiting beliefs, transform them into positive affirmations. For example, change "I will never have enough money" to "I am capable of attracting abundant resources."

4. Mirror Affirmations. Hold your notebook and look into the mirror. Recite each positive affirmation out loud while maintaining eye contact with your reflection. Feel the words resonate as you affirm your new beliefs about money and abundance.

5. Close the Ritual. After reciting your affirmations, express gratitude for this moment of insight and growth. You can keep the list of limiting beliefs and affirmations to refer back to regularly, reminding yourself of your journey toward financial empowerment.

Life Circumstances Clearing Ritual
Materials Needed:
- A piece of string or ribbon (preferably green or gold)
- A pair of scissors
- A quiet space
- A notepad or paper
Instructions:
1. Identify Financial Blocks. Begin by sitting in a quiet space with a notepad or paper, reflecting on

your current financial situation. Write down specific life circumstances that you believe are blocking your financial progress (e.g., job dissatisfaction, overspending, or lack of opportunities).

2. Create a Symbolic Knot. Once you have your list, take the string or ribbon and tie a knot for each blockage you identified, saying the corresponding circumstance as you tie each knot. For example, "This knot represents my dissatisfaction with my current job."

3. Cutting the String. After creating knots for each blockage, take a moment to visualize each blockage dissolving. Use the scissors to cut the string, symbolically severing those limitations from your life. As you cut, say:

"With this cut, I release control,

No longer shall these blocks take hold."

4. Dispose of the String. Discard the pieces of string outside, symbolizing the releasing of your financial obstacles. As you do this, visualize new opportunities and paths opening up before you.

5. Reflect and Move Forward. Take a moment to journal about any insights or feelings that came up during the ritual, and think about steps you can take to create a more abundant life.

Wealth Karma Cleansing Ritual
Materials Needed:
- A bowl of water

- A spoonful of salt (or sea salt)
- A white candle
- A quiet place

Instructions:

1. Prepare Your Space. Find a calm and peaceful area where you can sit comfortably. Arrange the bowl of water in front of you and place the candle nearby.

2. Purification Process. Light the white candle, which symbolizes purity and a fresh start. As the flame flickers, hold your hands over the bowl of water, and say:

"Water of life, cleanse my karma, restore my flow,

Free me from burdens, let abundance grow."

3. Add Salt for Purification. Carefully add the spoonful of salt to the water, stirring it gently. As you stir, visualize any negative karma or past actions that affect your financial situation being released into the water. Imagine the salt purifying and neutralizing those influences.

4. Reflective Meditation. Sit quietly for a moment and reflect on your financial behaviors and choices in the context of your karmic path. Consider what lessons and growth opportunities arise from these experiences.

5. Release with Gratitude. After your reflection, take a moment to pour the salted water onto the earth outside or down your drain as a symbol of releasing the past. Thank the universe for the lessons learned and affirm your commitment to creating positive

karma moving forward.

Techniques for Energy Clearing

Energy clearing is an essential practice for those seeking to enhance their financial prosperity and remove blockages that may hinder their abundance. One of the most effective techniques for energy clearing involves the use of crystals. Crystals such as citrine, pyrite, and green aventurine are known for their wealth-attracting properties. By placing these crystals in your workspace or carrying them in your pocket, you can create an energetic atmosphere conducive to financial growth. Additionally, cleansing these crystals regularly in moonlight or saltwater ensures they remain vibrant and effective in transmitting positive energy.

Another powerful method for clearing negative energy is candle magic. Using candles in colors associated with prosperity, such as green and gold, can amplify your intention when performing money spells. Light a candle while focusing on your financial goals, allowing the flame to symbolize the transformation of any blockages into positive energy. As you visualize your desires, the candle serves as a beacon, drawing in abundance and illuminating the path toward your prosperity.

Herbal sachets are also a traditional tool for attracting wealth and clearing stagnant energy. Blending herbs like cinnamon, basil, and mint creates a potent mix that can be placed in your home or carried with you. As you craft your sachets, infuse them with your intentions through affirmations and visualization, ensuring they resonate with your financial aspirations. The scents and energies of the herbs work together to dispel negativity, inviting prosperity into your life.

Moon phase rituals play a crucial role in aligning your energy with the natural cycles of abundance. Each phase of the moon offers unique opportunities for manifestation. For instance, the waxing phase is ideal for setting intentions and initiating new financial ventures, while the full moon is perfect for gratitude and reflection on your achievements. Engaging in rituals that honor these phases can help you harness lunar energy, enhancing your financial clarity and growth throughout the month.

Divination practices such as tarot or pendulum readings can provide insightful guidance on financial matters and help identify potential blockages. By connecting with your intuitive self, you can gain clarity on your relationship with money and uncover underlying beliefs that may be limiting your prosperity. Incorporating charms or talismans specifically designed for abundance can further support your energy clearing efforts. These items act as reminders of your intentions, reinforcing a mindset aligned with wealth and success, paving the way for a prosperous future.

Salt Bath Cleansing Ritual

Materials:

- Coarse sea salt or Epsom salt

- A bathtub (or large bowl for a foot soak)

- Optional: Essential oils (such as lavender or eucalyptus)

Instructions:

1. **Prepare the Bath:** Fill the bathtub with warm water, adding a generous amount of sea salt to cleanse away negativity. If using a bowl for a foot soak, fill it with warm water and add salt.

2. Set Your Intention. As the water fills, visualize any financial or abundance energy blocks dissolving into the water.

3. Add Essential Oils. If desired, add a few drops of essential oil to enhance the cleansing process and uplift your spirit.

4. Soak and Release. Immerse yourself in the water and relax for at least 20 minutes. During this time, focus on releasing any negative thoughts or beliefs about money. Envision yourself open and ready to receive prosperity.

5. Drain the Water. As you drain the bath, visualize all the blocks being washed away. You can also dispose of the water from the foot soak outside, symbolizing your release of negativity.

Smudging Ritual with Sage or Palo Santo
Materials Needed:
- Dried sage or palo santo stick
- A fireproof bowl or abalone shell
- Optional: A feather for wafting smoke
Instructions:

1. Create Your Sacred Space. Find a quiet area where you feel comfortable. Open windows to allow any negative energy to exit.

2. Light the Sage or Palo Santo. Carefully light the end of the sage or palo santo, allowing it to burn for a few moments before blowing out the flame, creating smoke.

3. Set Your Intention. As the smoke rises, hold your hands out and say:

   "With this smoke, I cleanse away,

   All blocks to abundance, let them not stay."

4. Waft the Smoke. Walk around your space, wafting the smoke toward your financial documents, wallet, and areas where you keep your money and resources. Envision the blocks lifting and making way for prosperity.

5. Conclude the Ritual. Once you've smudged the areas you wish to cleanse, extinguish the sage or palo santo safely and thank the plant for its energies.

Crystal Cleansing and Charging Ritual
Materials:
- Crystals (e.g., citrine, pyrite, green aventurine)

- A bowl of water (or saltwater)
- Optional: Brown rice (for longer cleansing)
Instructions:

1. Cleanse the Crystals. If using water, submerge your chosen crystals in the bowl of clean water for at least 30 minutes. If you prefer, you can use saltwater for more profound cleansing, but ensure the crystals are safe for water.

2. Charge the Crystals. After cleansing, place the crystals in sunlight or moonlight for a few hours to recharge them with positive energy.

3. Set Your Intention. Hold each crystal in your hand, focusing on your desires for abundance, prosperity, and opportunities. Say:

"With this crystal, I release all blocks,

I am open to wealth when prosperity knocks."

4. Use the Crystals. Carry the charged crystals with you, place them in your wallet, or keep them in your workspace to attract good fortune and keep your intention strong.

5. Regular Cleansing. Cleanse the crystals regularly (once a month) to maintain their potency in clearing blocks.

Visualization and Affirmation Ritual
Materials Needed.
- A quiet space
- A comfortable seat or cushion
- A pen and paper

Instructions:

1. Find Your Space. Sit comfortably in a quiet area where you can focus without distractions.

2. Write Your Blocks. On the piece of paper, list down any beliefs or feelings that may be blocking your abundance (e.g., "I fear spending money," "I believe I don't deserve financial success").

3. Set Your Affirmations. After identifying blocks, write positive affirmations that counter these beliefs, such as: "I am worthy of abundance," or "Money flows to me easily."

4. Meditate and Visualize. Close your eyes and take deep breaths. Visualize the energy of the blocks melting away, being replaced by light and positive energy. Affirm your new beliefs out loud while holding the paper.

5. Release the Paper. Once the visualization is complete, burn or bury the paper as a symbolic act of releasing those blocks, keeping your affirmations handy as a reminder of your new mindset.

Sound Cleansing Ritual with Bells or Singing Bowls

Materials:

- A bell, singing bowl, or any musical instrument that produces sound (like a drum or chimes)
- A quiet space

Instructions:

1. Choose Your Space. Find a calm and quiet area

where you can conduct your ritual without interruptions.

2. Set Your Intention. Before you begin, take a moment to focus on your intention—removing blocks to money, prosperity, luck, and opportunities.

3. Create a Sound Bath. Start by using the bell or singing bowl to create sound. If you have a singing bowl, gently strike it or rub the rim with a mallet until it sings. If using a bell, ring it steadily. As the sound resonates, visualize it washing over you like waves, clearing away all negativity and blockages to financial abundance.

4. Affirm with Sound. As you produce sound, speak or chant affirmations related to prosperity. For example:

"With this sound, I cleanse my way,

Removing all blocks, let abundance play."

Repeat this affirmation as you play the sound, allowing it to reverberate within your space.

5. Finish with Gratitude. After several minutes of sound cleansing, pause and sit in silence for a moment, feeling the residual energy of the sounds. Thank the universe or any spiritual guides you resonate with for supporting your journey toward abundance.

6. Integrate the Energy. You can also keep the instruments near areas where you handle money (like your wallet or financial documents) to help maintain a clear, open energy for prosperity.

Maintaining an Abundant Energy Flow

Maintaining an abundant energy flow is crucial for those seeking to harness prosperity magic in their lives. Understanding that energy is the foundation of all existence allows practitioners to tap into the forces that attract wealth and abundance. To begin, it's essential to cultivate a mindset that aligns with prosperity. This involves adopting beliefs that support abundance rather than scarcity. Affirmations play a significant role here; by regularly affirming one's worthiness of wealth and success, individuals can shift their internal narrative. Visualization techniques can also be employed to create a vivid mental picture of financial goals, making them feel more attainable and real.

Integrating physical tools can enhance the flow of abundant energy. Crystals such as citrine, pyrite, and green aventurine are renowned for their wealth-attracting properties. Carrying these stones or placing them strategically in your home or workspace can help amplify financial energies. Plus, candle magic is a powerful practice that can focus your intentions. Using green or gold candles during rituals can invoke the energy of prosperity, especially when combined with specific herbs like basil or cinnamon, which are known for their ability to attract wealth. Lighting these candles during significant lunar phases can further align your intentions with the natural rhythms of the universe.

Creating and maintaining a prosperity jar is another effective method to keep the energy flowing. This jar acts as a physical representation of your intentions and can include items such as coins, herbs, and personal affirmations. By regularly charging the jar with your energy and intentions, you ensure that it remains a vibrant source of wealth attraction. It's also beneficial to perform energy clearing rituals around your prosperity jar to remove any blockages that may hinder financial growth. Techniques such as smudging with sage or using sound bowls can help cleanse the space, allowing for a continuous flow of abundant energy.

Moon phase rituals are an ancient practice that can significantly influence financial growth. Each phase of the moon holds unique energies, and aligning your financial intentions with these cycles can enhance manifestation efforts. For instance, the new moon is ideal for setting intentions, while the full moon is perfect for gratitude and releasing any limiting beliefs about money. By syncing your rituals with these lunar phases, you can cultivate an environment rich in prosperity energy, making it easier to attract the wealth and resources you desire.

Incorporating divination practices can provide valuable insights into your financial journey. Tarot or rune readings can reveal hidden blockages or opportunities that may not be immediately apparent.

Using charms and talismans for abundance can further reinforce your intentions. These items serve as constant reminders of your goals and can be charged with specific energies to enhance their effectiveness. By consistently engaging in these practices, you create a dynamic and abundant energy flow that supports your financial aspirations, paving the way for a prosperous future.

Daily Gratitude and Visualization Ritual

Materials:

- A notebook or gratitude journal
- A pen
- A quiet space
- Optional: A small bowl or container for gratitude notes

Instructions:

1. Set Aside Time. Dedicate a few minutes each day, ideally in the morning or evening, when you can focus uninterrupted.

2. Write Your Gratitude. Begin by writing down at least three things you are grateful for in your life. These can be related to money, opportunities, relationships, or anything that brings you joy. Focus on specific details to enhance your feelings of appreciation.

3. Visualization Your Abundant Life. After writing, close your eyes and take a few deep breaths. Visualize your life filled with abundance, imagining the

feelings of security, happiness, and fulfillment that come with it. Picture opportunities flowing naturally to you, as well as financial resources being readily available.

4. Create Gratitude Notes. If you wish, write short gratitude notes reflecting on moments of abundance throughout the week and place them in a bowl or container. You can periodically read them to reinforce positive energy.

5. Close the Ritual. End your practice with an affirmation, such as:

"I am a magnet for abundance,
Opportunities flow to me effortlessly.
I attract all that I need for my highest good."

Abundance Flow Jar Ritual

Materials Needed:

- A clear jar or container
- Small items that represent abundance (e.g., coins, dried flowers, herbs like basil or chamomile)
- A piece of paper
- A pen
- Optional: A green or gold candle

Instructions:

1. Create the Abundance Jar. Start by finding a dedicated jar or container that inspires you. Cleanse it by washing it in saltwater or giving it a good rinse, symbolically starting fresh.

2. Choose Your Abundance Items. Gather small

items that symbolize abundance for you. This could include coins, crystals (like citrine), or dried herbs (basil for prosperity, chamomile for calmness). Fill the jar with these items as you focus on your intention to attract and maintain the flow of abundance energy.

3. Write Your Intention. On a small piece of paper, write a statement about your intention for abundance. For instance: "I maintain the flow of abundance in my life, welcoming opportunities and prosperity."

4. Add to the Jar. Fold the piece of paper and place it at the bottom of the jar before filling it with other abundance items, sealing your intention within the jar.

5. Charge the Jar with Energy. If you'd like, you can place a green or gold candle next to the jar. Light the candle and visualize vibrant energy radiating from the jar, filling your environment with positive abundance. Repeat the affirmation:

"Abundance surrounds me, it flows and grows,
With this jar, my prosperity knows no lows."

6. Keep the Jar Visible. Place the jar in a prominent spot in your home where you'll see it regularly. This will serve as a physical reminder of your intention and the flow of abundance in your life. You can also add more items periodically to amplify this energy.

Protective Magic for Sustained Success

Spells to Guard Against Financial Troubles

Warding and protection spells are essential tools in the practice of prosperity magic, particularly for those seeking to keep negative energy and financial troubles at bay. In the modern context, where economic fluctuations can create uncertainty and stress, these spells serve as proactive measures to create a shield against harmful influences. By harnessing the energy around us, practitioners can cultivate a protective barrier that not only safeguards their finances but also fosters an environment conducive to abundance and wealth attraction.

One of the most effective methods of warding off negative energy involves the use of crystals known for their protective properties. Crystals such as black tourmaline, amethyst, and citrine can be strategically placed around your home or workspace to absorb negativity and promote positive energy flow. Combining these stones with affirmations can amplify their effectiveness. For instance, regularly reciting affirmations focused on wealth and protection while holding or placing the crystals can enhance your intentions, ensuring that your financial aspirations are not hindered by outside forces.

Candle magic is another powerful tool in the realm of warding and protection. By choosing specific colors that correspond to your intentions—green for wealth, black for protection, and white for clarity—you can create a focused ritual. Lighting candles during the waxing moon phase, when energies are rising, can be particularly potent. As you light the candle, visualize a protective shield surrounding your financial goals, effectively blocking out any unwanted energies that could impede your progress. Allow the candle to burn completely, knowing that the energy you've put into the ritual will continue to work on your behalf.

Incorporating herbal sachets into your practice also offers a tangible way to repel negativity while attracting wealth. Herbs such as basil, cinnamon, and rosemary are known for their prosperity-enhancing properties. By creating sachets filled with these herbs and placing them in your home or carrying them with you, you can create a constant reminder of your intentions while keeping financial troubles at bay. Additionally, these sachets can be charged during specific moon phases, enhancing their potency and aligning them with the natural rhythms of abundance and growth.

Adding energy clearing practices is beneficial for maintaining a prosperous environment. Regularly cleansing your space with sage, palo santo, or sound vibrations can remove any lingering negative energies that might block financial growth. Pairing this with divination practices, such as tarot or pendulum readings, can provide insight into any potential blockages and guide you in adjusting your strategies. By committing to these protective rituals, you create a space where abundance can flow freely, allowing you to attract wealth and maintain a prosperous mindset amidst the challenges of modern life.

Prosperity Shielding and Continued Financial Growth

Prosperity shielding is an essential aspect of ensuring continued financial growth, especially for those who embrace the principles of prosperity magic. One of the most effective techniques in this realm is the use of crystal energy. Certain crystals, such as citrine, pyrite, and green aventurine, are renowned for their ability to attract wealth and abundance. By incorporating these stones into your daily life—whether by wearing them as jewelry, placing them on your workspace, or creating a crystal grid—you can amplify your financial intentions. Regularly cleansing and charging these crystals under the moonlight enhances their potency, allowing them to serve as powerful allies in your quest for financial prosperity.

Money manifestation rituals represent another critical technique for shielding your prosperity. These rituals can be tailored to suit your personal beliefs and practices. A popular method involves writing down specific financial goals and desires on a piece of paper, then performing a ritual to release these intentions into the universe. This could include lighting a green candle while visualizing your goals being achieved or creating a vision board that visually represents your aspirations. Engaging in these practices not only focuses your energy on attracting wealth but also cultivates a mindset oriented toward abundance, further solidifying your financial trajectory.

Including herbal sachets in your prosperity shielding routine is another potent technique. Herbs such as basil, cinnamon, and chamomile are traditionally associated with wealth attraction. You can create sachets filled with these herbs and place them in your wallet, business space, or under your pillow to invite financial opportunities. Additionally, these herbal sachets can be charged with specific intentions, further enhancing their effectiveness. By connecting with the natural world and its abundant energies, you align yourself with the vibrations of prosperity, ensuring a continuous flow of financial growth.

The lunar cycle offers profound opportunities for financial rituals, as each phase of the moon carries distinct energies. During the waxing phase, when the moon is growing, it is an ideal time for setting intentions related to wealth and abundance. Conversely, the waning phase can be utilized for releasing limiting beliefs and financial blockages. By aligning your financial practices with the moon phases, you can create a rhythm of growth and release that keeps your financial situation in a state of flux, optimizing your prosperity potential. Engaging with these natural cycles not only enhances your financial well-being but also deepens your connection to the universe.

Energy clearing techniques play a crucial role in shielding your prosperity. Regularly cleansing your space, whether through smudging with sage or using sound healing methods, helps remove negative energies that may hinder your financial growth. Additionally, incorporating divination practices, such as tarot or pendulum readings, can provide insights into your financial situation, revealing areas for improvement and affirming your path toward abundance. Charms and talismans can also be effective tools in this regard, serving as physical reminders of your prosperity intentions. By combining these techniques, you create a robust framework for shielding your prosperity, ensuring that your financial growth remains steady and vibrant.

Four-Leaf Clover Protection Spell

Materials Needed:

- A small dish or bowl
- Dried herbs (such as basil and mint for prosperity)
- A fresh or dried four-leaf clover, or a symbolic representation (ex. a jewelry charm)
- A coin (for luck)

Instructions:

1. Place the dried herbs in the dish as a base for the spell, symbolizing growth and abundance.
2. Add the four-leaf clover on top of the herbs and place the coin next to it, representing luck.
3. As you arrange the items, say, "With this clover, I attract luck and financial opportunities into my life."
4. Leave the dish in a prominent spot to symbolize the constant flow of luck and prosperity coming to you.
5. Each morning, repeat your affirmation while focusing on the dish, reinforcing your intent for prosperity and good fortune.

Money Protection Spell

Materials:

- A small green or gold pouch (for prosperity)
- A few coins (preferably of various denominations)
- A sprig of dried mint or basil (known for attracting and protecting money)

- A piece of paper
- A pen

Instructions:

1. Prepare Your Space. Find a quiet area where you can focus without distractions. Begin by cleansing your space energetically through visualization or by lighting a candle.

2. Write Your Intention. On the piece of paper, write a statement that affirms your desire to protect your financial resources. For example: "I am safe, my money is secure, and my prosperity is protected."

3. Gather Your Items. Place the coins and the sprig of mint or basil into the pouch as you focus on your intention of safeguarding your wealth.

4. Charge the Pouch. Hold the pouch in your hands and visualize a bright green or golden light enveloping it. As you do this, say the following affirmation:

"This pouch contains my wealth and more,
Protected from harm, it shall soar.
Abundance surrounds, and it safely stays,
Guarded by light in all of my days."

5. Keep the Pouch Close. Carry the pouch in your wallet, handbag, or keep it in a secure place at home, such as a safe or on your altar. Whenever you interact with it, remember your intention for protection.

Guardian of Wealth Ritual

Materials:

- A small bowl
- Holly leaves (for protection)
- Sage or rosemary (for cleansing)
- A coin or small bill

Instructions:

1. Place the coin or bill in the bowl as a representation of your financial assets.

2. Add the holly leaves around the coin to create a protective barrier.

3. Burn the sage or rosemary, allowing the smoke to cleanse and protect the bowl's contents.

4. As the smoke envelops the bowl, recite, "With this smoke, I protect my wealth. It is safe and secure from harm."

5. Leave the bowl undisturbed for 24 hours, then place it in a secure area of your home to maintain protective energy.

Prosperous Home Protection Spell

Materials:

- A small bowl of salt (for purification and protection)
- A small bowl of water (to symbolize clarity)
- A small green candle (for prosperity)
- A piece of string or ribbon (green or gold)
- A piece of paper
- A pen

Instructions:

1. Create Your Ritual Space. Set up a small altar or

table where you can place the bowls, candle, and materials. Make sure this space feels sacred and quiet.

2. Write Your Intention. On the piece of paper, write an intention stating your desire to protect the prosperity in your home. For example: "My home is safe, my prosperity is secure, and my resources are protected."

3. Set Up the Bowls. Place the bowl of salt next to the bowl of water. As you do this, say:

"Salt for protection, water for clarity,

Together they nurture my prosperity."

4. Light the Candle. Light the green candle, visualizing it drawing abundance while also casting a protective glow over your home.

5. Wrap and Secure. Take the piece of string or ribbon and wrap it around the bowls, placing them together while saying:

"This string I bind, protection and grace,

My home is a haven, a safe, sacred space."

6. Place the Paper. After wrapping, place the written intention under the bowls. Allow the candle to burn for a while as you focus on your intention.

7. Conclude the Ritual. Once the candle has burned down or you feel ready, dispose of the salt and water in your garden or safe place outside, symbolizing the establishment of protective energy around your home. Keep the paper in a special place to remind you of your commitment to maintaining the safety of your prosperity.

Integrating Prosperity Magic into Daily Life

Building a Prosperity Mindset

Building a prosperity mindset is an essential step for anyone looking to attract wealth and abundance into their lives. At its core, a prosperity mindset involves not just a positive attitude towards money, but a deep-seated belief that financial success is both achievable and deserved. This mindset acts as a foundation for various practices in prosperity magic, enabling individuals to align their thoughts, emotions, and actions with their financial goals. By understanding and cultivating a prosperity mindset, witches and spiritual seekers can enhance their ability to manifest wealth and transform their financial reality.

To cultivate this mindset, it is crucial to start by examining and challenging any limiting beliefs about money. Many people carry negative narratives about wealth, often rooted in societal conditioning or personal experiences. Engaging in self-reflection through journaling or meditation can help identify these beliefs. Once recognized, they can be reframed using abundance affirmations. Phrases like "I am worthy of wealth" or "Money flows to me effortlessly" can replace self-doubt and fear, reinforcing a more positive and empowering perspective on financial abundance.

Visualization techniques play a significant role in building a prosperity mindset. By vividly imagining the life one desires, including financial stability and the luxuries that come with it, individuals can create a strong emotional connection to their goals. This mental imagery not only motivates action but also sends a clear signal to the universe about one's intentions. Incorporating this practice into a daily routine, perhaps alongside candle magic or moon phase rituals, can amplify the intention behind the visualization, making it a powerful tool for manifestation.

Energy clearing is another important aspect of developing a prosperity mindset. Many people unknowingly carry energetic blockages that hinder their financial growth. Techniques such as smudging with herbs, using sound vibrations, or working with crystals can help to cleanse these energies. This process creates a more receptive state for abundance, allowing individuals to attract wealth without the interference of past traumas or negative patterns. Regularly engaging in energy clearing practices can maintain a mindset that is open to receiving prosperity.

Blending practical actions with spiritual practices solidifies the prosperity mindset. This can include creating prosperity jars filled with symbols of wealth, utilizing herbal sachets for attracting abundance, or engaging in divination practices to gain insight into financial opportunities. By blending the tangible with the spiritual, individuals can reinforce their commitment to financial growth. This holistic approach not only enhances the effectiveness of money spells and rituals but also instills a deeper sense of confidence and purpose in the pursuit of prosperity.

Golden Coin Prosperity Gratitude Spell

Materials:
- A small dish or bowl
- A gold coin or token
- A piece of brown or green paper
- A pen

Instructions:

1. On the brown or green paper, write down three things you are grateful for in your current life.

2. Place the gold coin in the dish and surround it with the meaningful things you wrote.

3. Hold your hands over the dish and say, "With gratitude, I attract luxury and abundance into my life."

4. Leave the dish in a prominent place for one week, enhancing your focus on comfort and luxury.

5. At the end of the week, thank the universe for the blessings received and continue your gratitude practice.

Gratitude Jar Ritual

Materials Needed:

- A jar or container (clear glass works well)

- Small pieces of paper or gratitude notes

- A pen

- Optional: Decorative items (like ribbons or stickers) to personalize the jar

Instructions:

1. Prepare the Jar. Decorate the jar as you wish, making it visually appealing. This will serve as your sacred space for gratitude.

2. Set Your Intention. Sit quietly for a moment and focus on your intention to cultivate a mindset of abundance and recognize the prosperity you already have in your life.

3. Write Gratitude Notes. Each day, write down at least one thing you are grateful for regarding your financial situation or abundance in general. Examples might include your job, supportive relationships, or other resources.

4. Fill the Jar. Fold each note and place it in the jar. As you do this, say a small affirmation like:

"With this note, I acknowledge my gain,

Abundance surrounds me, I will not restrain."

5. Reflect and Read. At the end of each week or month, read through the notes in the jar. Reflect on how far you have come in your mindset. This will reinforce your gratitude for existing abundance and help you focus on prosperity moving forward.

Affirmation and Visualization Ritual

Materials Needed:

- A comfortable and quiet space

- A mirror (full-length or handheld)

- A list of affirmations related to prosperity (you can create your own or use the ones below)

Instructions:

1. Choose Your Time. Set aside a specific time each day (like morning or evening) to perform this ritual.

2. Create Your Affirmations. Write down powerful affirmations that resonate with you and your financial goals. Examples include:

  - "I am worthy of abundance and financial success."

  - "Money flows easily into my life."

  - "I attract opportunities for prosperity."

3. Stand Before the Mirror. Stand in front of the mirror and take a few deep breaths to center yourself. Look into your eyes and project confidence and positivity.

4. Recite Your Affirmations. Speak each affirmation out loud while maintaining eye contact with yourself. Visualize the energy of your affirmations manifesting

in your life. Feel the emotions associated with achieving your financial goals.

5. Close the Ritual. End your practice by thanking yourself for the journey toward a prosperity mindset. Commit to repeating this ritual daily, allowing the affirmations to deepen your belief in abundance.

Wealth Visualization Meditation

Materials:

- A quiet space where you won't be disturbed
- Comfortable clothing
- Optional: Soothing music or nature sounds

Instructions:

1. Create a Calm Environment. Find a comfortable spot to sit or lie down. If preferred, play soothing music or nature sounds to enhance relaxation.

2. Ground Yourself. Begin with a few deep breaths. Inhale deeply through your nose, hold for a moment, and then exhale slowly through your mouth. Allow any tension to release from your body.

3. Visualize Abundance. Close your eyes and imagine a scene where you are experiencing financial abundance. Picture yourself in a setting that represents your ideal financial life. This could be enjoying an experience, traveling, or living in your dream home.

4. Engage Your Senses. As you visualize, engage all your senses. What do you see? Hear? Feel? Smell? The more vividly you can imagine this scenario, the

stronger it will resonate with your subconscious.

5. Stay in the Visualization. Remain in this meditative state for 5-10 minutes, absorbing the feelings of contentment, joy, and security that come from visualizing prosperity.

6. Gratitude and Release. Once you are ready, bring your awareness back to the present moment. Take a few deep breaths, expressing gratitude for your ability to attract abundance. Commit to taking inspired actions that align with your vision of prosperity.

Daily Practices for Abundance

Daily practices for abundance are essential for creating a mindset and environment conducive to prosperity. For those engaged in witchcraft and spiritual exploration, incorporating rituals and affirmations into everyday life can significantly enhance the flow of wealth and opportunities. One of the simplest yet most effective practices is to start each day with positive affirmations focused on abundance. This could involve stating affirmations such as "I am worthy of financial success" or "Wealth flows to me effortlessly." By consistently repeating these affirmations, you align your energy with the vibrations of prosperity, attracting more positive financial outcomes into your life.

Visualization techniques also play a crucial role in manifesting abundance. Set aside a few minutes each morning to visualize your financial goals. Picture yourself living in a state of abundance—imagine the details of your desired lifestyle, the feelings associated with financial freedom, and the opportunities that come your way. Visualization serves to create a mental image of success, helping to rewire your subconscious mind to recognize and seize opportunities that align with your financial aspirations. Incorporating this practice into your daily routine can significantly enhance your ability to attract wealth.

Candle magic is another powerful tool for those seeking financial prosperity. Each week, choose a color associated with abundance—green for growth, gold for wealth, or even purple for spiritual prosperity. Carve your intentions into the candle or dress it with oils and herbs known for attracting wealth, such as cinnamon or basil. As you light the candle, focus on your intentions and the energy you wish to draw into your life. This ritual not only serves as a reminder of your goals but also creates a sacred space for your intentions to manifest.

Integrating herbal sachets into your daily life can further enhance your abundance practices. Create a sachet filled with herbs like chamomile, mint, or patchouli, which are often associated with attracting wealth. Carry this sachet with you or place it in your workspace to create a constant energetic reminder of your intentions. The scent and energy of the herbs will serve to uplift your spirits and attract positive financial energy throughout your day.

Consider aligning your abundance practices with the moon phases. Each phase of the moon can be harnessed for different aspects of financial growth. During the waxing moon, focus on setting intentions and attracting wealth; during the full moon, perform rituals to celebrate financial achievements and release what no longer serves you. By tuning into the natural rhythms of the moon, you can enhance your financial manifestations and create a deeper connection with the universal energies that support your journey toward abundance.

Luck, Gambling Spells, and Ethics

Luck and gambling spells can be alluring for those seeking quick financial gains, but it is essential to approach these practices with a sense of ethics and responsibility. As witches and spiritual seekers, we are often drawn to the idea of attracting wealth and fortune through spells and rituals. However, the potential impact of our actions on ourselves and others must be carefully considered. Engaging in practices that manipulate luck or fortunes can lead to unintended consequences, and it is crucial to maintain a balanced perspective on the energy we are inviting into our lives.

One method for responsible practice is to set clear intentions before casting any luck or gambling spells.

This involves not only defining what you wish to achieve but also recognizing the potential ramifications of your desires. For instance, seeking wealth through gambling can lead to addiction or financial instability if not approached with caution. By focusing on intentions that emphasize abundance and prosperity in holistic ways—such as through hard work, creativity, and ethical investments—we align ourselves with positive energies that enhance our overall financial well-being without compromising our values.

Including wealth and abundance affirmations and visualization techniques can also serve as a responsible approach to attracting wealth. Instead of relying solely on luck, practitioners can harness the power of their minds to manifest financial success. Visualizing oneself in a state of abundance while affirming positive beliefs about wealth can create a strong energetic foundation for prosperity. This method empowers individuals to take control of their financial destinies through their actions, reinforcing the idea that they are active participants in their journeys rather than passive recipients of luck.

Also, utilizing tools like crystals, candle magic, and herbal sachets can enhance one's financial practice while maintaining ethical standards. For example, using citrine or pyrite in wealth-attraction spells can promote positive energy and abundance without the risks associated with gambling. Similarly, candle magic can be employed to focus intentions on prosperity while inviting protective energies that shield against financial loss. By integrating these practices, individuals can cultivate a richer financial landscape that aligns with their ethical beliefs.

The use of divination practices for financial insight can provide clarity and guidance on when and how to engage in luck-based ventures. Tarot readings or other forms of divination enable practitioners to assess their current financial situations and make informed decisions about pursuing luck through gambling or similar activities. By maintaining a clear understanding of one's financial circumstances and the associated risks, witches can navigate the complex interplay of luck and intention with greater wisdom, fostering a responsible and ethical approach to prosperity magic.

Creating a Supportive Environment for Wealth

Creating a supportive environment for wealth involves cultivating both your physical space and your mental landscape. Start by decluttering your surroundings. A clean and organized environment allows positive energy to flow freely, making room for prosperity to enter your life. Remove items that do not serve your financial goals or bring you joy. Surround yourself with symbols of abundance, such as plants, crystals like citrine or pyrite, and images that inspire wealth creation. Each element in your space should resonate with your intention of attracting prosperity.

Using prosperity magic in your daily routine can significantly enhance your financial environment. Consider setting up a prosperity jar filled with items that symbolize abundance, such as coins, herbs like basil and cinnamon, and affirmations written on paper. Place this jar in a prominent location in your home to serve as a constant reminder of your wealth goals. Additionally, you can utilize candle magic by lighting green or gold candles during rituals that focus on financial growth. As the candle burns, visualize your goals coming to fruition, allowing the flame to amplify your intentions.

Engaging with the cycles of the moon can also support your wealth-building efforts. The new moon is an excellent time for setting intentions and beginning new financial ventures, while the full moon can be a moment for gratitude and reflection on what you have achieved so far. During these phases, perform rituals that align with your financial aspirations, such as writing down your goals, creating abundance affirmations, or conducting visualization techniques that clearly depict your desired financial reality. The natural rhythms of the moon can provide a powerful backdrop for your prosperity work.

In addition to rituals, consider using herbal sachets and charms as tools for attracting wealth. Create sachets that include herbs known for their money-attracting properties, such as mint, chamomile, and ginger. Place these sachets in your wallet, purse, or workspace to continuously draw in financial opportunities. Similarly, charms and talismans can be carried or worn to enhance your personal allure to wealth. Choose symbols that resonate with your beliefs and intentions, ensuring they serve as reminders of your commitment to financial abundance.

Regular energy clearing practices can help remove any blockages that may hinder your financial growth. Techniques such as smudging with sage or using sound healing can cleanse your environment and personal energy field. This creates a fertile ground for your wealth intentions to take root. Additionally, incorporating divination practices—like tarot readings focused on financial insight—can provide clarity and guidance on your journey. By combining these practices, you create a holistic approach to fostering a supportive environment for wealth, empowering you to manifest the prosperity you desire.

Online Communities and Support Groups

Online communities and support groups have become essential spaces for individuals seeking to enhance their understanding and practice of prosperity magic. These digital platforms foster connection among like-minded witches, pagans, and spiritual seekers, offering a wealth of resources and shared experiences. Engaging in these communities allows members to exchange ideas about money spells, abundance rituals, and various techniques for manifesting wealth. With the rise of social media and online forums, it is easier than ever for practitioners from different backgrounds and regions to come together and support one another on their journeys toward financial abundance.

One of the primary benefits of participating in online communities is the access to diverse perspectives and practices. Members can share their experiences with specific rituals, such as candle magic for financial prosperity or using herbal sachets to attract wealth. This exchange of knowledge can help individuals refine their own practices, learn new techniques, and gain inspiration from others' successes. Additionally, many groups host workshops or discussions led by experienced practitioners, providing invaluable guidance on topics like moon phase rituals for financial growth or the effective use of prosperity jars.

These online platforms also serve as spaces for emotional support and encouragement. The path to financial prosperity can often feel isolating, especially for those who might not have a supportive network in their immediate surroundings. By connecting with others who share similar aspirations, individuals can find camaraderie and motivation. Sharing personal stories about overcoming financial challenges or celebrating small victories can help create a sense of community and belonging, essential for fostering resilience in the face of obstacles.

Online communities are rich resources for practical tools and rituals that promote financial well-being. Many groups share guides on creating abundance affirmations, visualization techniques, and even divination practices for financial insight. Members can access a range of materials, from templates for prosperity jars to recipes for energy-clearing herbal blends. These resources empower individuals to take actionable steps toward their financial goals while reinforcing the belief that they have the power to attract abundance into their lives.

The dynamic nature of online communities allows for continuous growth and adaptation. As prosperity magic evolves, so too do the practices and techniques shared within these groups. New trends, such as the integration of crystals for wealth attraction or the use of charms and talismans for abundance, can gain traction and inspire fresh ideas. By staying engaged with these communities, practitioners can keep their practices aligned with current trends while also contributing their unique insights, thereby enriching the collective knowledge and fostering a spirit of collaboration in the pursuit of prosperity.

Workshops and Courses for Deeper Knowledge

Workshops and courses dedicated to prosperity magic provide an invaluable resource for those seeking to deepen their understanding of wealth attraction and financial growth. These educational experiences cater to a diverse audience, including witches, pagans, spiritual seekers, and entrepreneurs from various generations. By participating in these workshops, individuals can tap into the collective knowledge and practices that have been passed down through generations, allowing them to refine their abilities in money spells, abundance rituals, and financial manifestations.

One of the most beneficial aspects of workshops is the opportunity for hands-on learning. Attendees can engage in practical exercises that demonstrate the effectiveness of various techniques, such as candle magic for financial prosperity and the creation of prosperity jars. Instructors often guide participants through the process of crafting herbal sachets designed to attract wealth and prosperity, incorporating herbs known for their financial-enhancing properties. This immersive approach not only solidifies understanding but also fosters a supportive community where participants can share experiences and insights.

Courses often delve into the specific nuances of financial rituals aligned with lunar phases, teaching practitioners how to harness the energy of the moon to enhance their wealth attraction efforts. Understanding the timing and energy of each moon phase can greatly influence the effectiveness of money manifestation rituals. These courses typically include divination practices, helping students gain financial insight through tarot readings, pendulum work, or other forms of divination, empowering them to make informed decisions in their financial journeys.

Abundance affirmations and visualization techniques are frequently explored within these educational settings, as they play a crucial role in shaping a prosperous mindset. Workshops may involve guided meditations and vision board creations, encouraging participants to visualize their financial goals and affirm their worthiness of abundance. By reinforcing positive beliefs about money and success, attendees can overcome limiting beliefs that may be hindering their financial growth.

Energy clearing practices are essential components of many prosperity-focused workshops. Participants learn to identify and remove financial blockages that may stem from past experiences or inherited beliefs. Techniques such as smudging, crystal work, and sound healing are often employed to facilitate this clearing process. By addressing these energetic obstacles, individuals can create a more receptive environment for prosperity to flow into their lives, leading to enhanced financial well-being and abundance.

About the Author

Emeleth Morliniel has been practicing witchcraft for more than thirty years. She is an intuitive astrologer, a certified Wiccan practitioner coach, an energy worker, and holds a Third Degree in British Celtic Traditional Witchcraft. That's a fancy way of saying she underwent a lot of education and elevation rites, and is now considered qualified to be a High Priestess. Within her own Circle, she's usually the one managing the group's energy work and spellcraft because she's exceedingly bad at memorizing lines.